That's SNEAKY!

CRISPIN BOYER

NATIONAL
GEOGRAPHIC

WASHINGTON, D.C.

SNEAKY
Contents

Meet Your Sneaky Host!

Meet Your Sneaky Host!

PSSST. WANNA HEAR A SECRET? HOW ABOUT A FEW HUNDRED OF 'EM?

Maybe a mustache-grooming tip, to boot? You've come to the right place! Welcome to *That's Sneaky!*, a collection of classified facts and cases of cunning hosted by yours truly, Secret Agent 'Stache. What makes me the perfect MC for everything sneaky (well, aside from my magnificent mustache)? I've spent the past two decades deep undercover as an agent for P.S.S.S.T.—the Professional Sleuths of Super-Secret Truths. You'd be amazed at the stuff people say when they see my trustworthy lip whiskers! Secrets were my stock-in-trade—until the P.S.S.S.T.'s top brass instituted a strict ban on facial hair. The nerve of those baby-faced desk jockeys!

Now I'm a rogue agent, ready to tell all—but only to you! Prepare to meet supreme sneaks of both the human and wildlife varieties, including a crab that creates its own costumes, "food stylists" who fashion phony feasts, and escape-plotting prisoners who built a glider right under the noses of their captors. You'll find ninja warriors and con artists, dashing spies and masters of disguise, funny money and phony photography, magicians' tricks and the secrets behind movie magic, trapdoors and trap-door spiders. You'll learn how to run your own spy network, communicate in code, and detect scams and hidden advertising. By the time you close the book on *That's Sneaky!*, you'll practically be a member of P.S.S.S.T. yourself! And you don't even need to know the secret handshake or abide by their ridiculous regulations regarding facial hair!

SECRET AGENT 'STACHE

How to Get the Most From
That's SNEAKY!

STEP 1:
WATCH OUT!

As you slink through *That's Sneaky!*, keep an eye peeled for these fun features...

PRIVATE EYES: Ten of these sneaky peepers lurk in each chapter (except Chapter 8), hidden in photos or creeping across the pages. Some are obvious; most are not. Can you spot them all? Check out page 175 for the answers.

SNEAK PEEKS: These galleries offer an unauthorized glimpse of secret spaces and stealthy techniques.

SNEAKY EQUIPMENT: Roundups of gear essential to stealth are scattered throughout *That's Sneaky!*

'STACHE'S SECRETS: Before he went rogue from the Professional Sleuths of Super-Secret Truths, Agent 'Stache swiped some of the organization's most sensitive information. Watch for the whiskered one to surface from the shadows and share bonus bits of uncommon knowledge.

STEP 2: KNOW YOUR STEALTHY TERMINOLOGY!

This book is full of terms that rarely pop up in your everyday life. If you're ever stumped about the meaning of a word, flip back to this glossary for a fast refresher.

CIPHER: A code for replacing or rearranging letters to create secret messages.

CLANDESTINE: A secret or sneaky way of conducting an activity.

COMMANDO: An elite soldier specializing in secret operations behind enemy lines.

CON ARTIST: Someone who tries to scam victims out of their valuables.

DOUBLE AGENT: A spy who pretends to work for one agency while secretly helping another.

ESPIONAGE: The act of spying, or gathering information on another person or country in secret.

HACKER: A tech expert who tries to gain unauthorized access to computers.

INFILTRATION: The act of slipping into a building or country without being detected.

MERCENARY: A warrior who works for the highest bidder.

MIMIC: An animal that copies the appearance or behavior of another animal to survive.

SHINOBI: Another word for a ninja.

SPY: A person who gathers information from another government or organization in secret.

STEP 3: GET READY TO RATE!

During his years as a seeker of sneaky phenomena, Secret Agent 'Stache developed the SHHH Scale—or Spectrum of Hush-Hush Hierarchy—to measure degrees of sneakiness. The higher he ranks something on the scale, the sneakier it is! You'll find these ratings at the end of each chapter. If you disagree with them, make your own SHHH Scale and poll your pals!

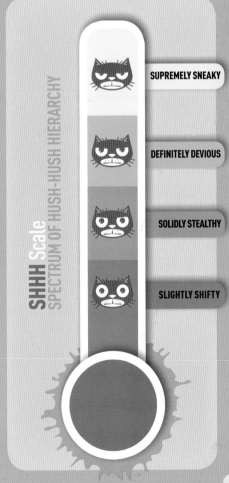

SHHH Scale
SPECTRUM OF HUSH-HUSH HIERARCHY

SUPREMELY SNEAKY

DEFINITELY DEVIOUS

SOLIDLY STEALTHY

SLIGHTLY SHIFTY

AUTHORIZED PERSONNEL ONLY BEYOND THIS POINT

VERIFY IDENTITY TO PROCEED

FINGERPRINT IDENTIFICATION

PLEASE PLACE YOUR RIGHT INDEX FINGER ON THE SCANNER.

RETINA SCAN

PLEASE LOOK INTO THE SCANNER WITH YOUR RIGHT EYE. TRY NOT TO BLINK FOR FIVE SECONDS.

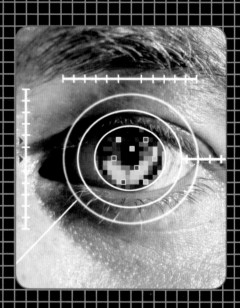

ACCESS GRANTED

ACCESS GRANTED

ACCESS DENIED

ACCESS DENIED

IDENTITY SUCCESSFULLY VERIFIED
YOU MAY NOW ACCESS *THAT'S SNEAKY!*
THIS BOOK IS FOR YOUR EYES ONLY

VOICE-PRINT IDENTIFICATION

PLEASE STATE YOUR NAME CLEARLY INTO THE MICROPHONE.

FACE-RECOGNITION SCAN

LOOK AT THE SCANNING SCREEN FOR FIVE SECONDS. DO NOT SMILE OR BLINK, PLEASE.

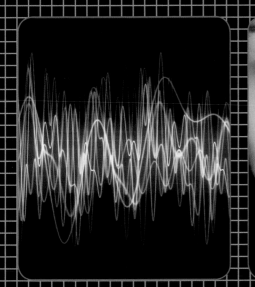

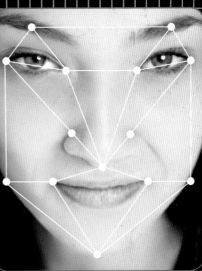

ACCESS GRANTED

ACCESS DENIED

ACCESS GRANTED

ACCESS DENIED

CHAPTER 1

Wild
and Wily

YOU WON'T SEE THE WORLD'S GREATEST ACTORS AND BEST COSTUMES ON THE ACADEMY AWARDS. They're behind the scenes—or behind the scenery—on land, under the sea, and in the air. This chapter reveals the wiliest tricks of wildlife, from the deceptive "dress" of camouflage to outstanding animal performances. If you think people take the top prize for sneakiness, then get ready for a new perspective on predators, prey, and even your pet!

PEAK SNEAKS: FIVE SLY PREDATORS

LEOPARDS

WHERE THEY LIVE: THE SOUTHERN HALF OF AFRICA, ACROSS ASIA, AND IN INDIA

THEIR SECRET WEAPON: SUPER STEALTH

The impala never saw it coming. In a blur of spotted fur, a leopard pounced from the brush just feet away. The cat had been stalking the impala all evening, crawling on its belly to stay low to the ground and blend in with tall grass. Silently, patiently, it crept closer until it was time to strike.

The stealthiest of the so-called "big cats"—a classification that includes lions, tigers, and jaguars—leopards stalk with the grace of much smaller felines, tiptoeing on the pads of their paws and creeping ghostlike through the brush until close enough to pounce on prey. Their spotted fur blends with trees, grass, and shadows, making the animal nearly invisible. Able to see better in the dark than lions and tigers, leopards do much of their hunting at night. In fact, leopards are so elusive that scientists have a hard time studying these solitary animals.

When in doubt, leopard researchers in some parts of the world simply look up. No big cat is more at home in a tree than a leopard. Some will even curl their tails around branches to help them hang on. The cats scramble skyward not only to hide prey from scavengers or escape from lions—they also mount attacks from tree limbs, pouncing on unsuspecting prey below.

CONE SNAILS

WHERE THEY LIVE: CORAL REEFS IN THE INDO-PACIFIC

THEIR SECRET WEAPON: TOXIC STING

Slow and steady might win the race for snails on land, but a group of aquatic gastropods called cone snails takes a different approach to survival: slow and deadly! These six-inch (15-cm) snails creep along the seafloor at night, sniffing out snoozing fish (awake fish dart away too quickly). Once it finds its victim, a cone snail engulfs it with a tubelike mouth and flushes a sort of sleeping potion over the fish's gills. Trapped in its worst nightmare, the paralyzed fish sits helpless until the cone snail jabs it with a harpoonlike tooth that injects a lethal toxin.

ANGLERFISH

WHERE THEY LIVE: A MILE (1.6 KM) DEEP IN THE ATLANTIC AND ANTARCTIC OCEANS

THEIR SECRET WEAPON: BUILT-IN FISHING ROD

This ugly lurker of the deep is proof that looks really can kill. Female members of the species have a special spine on top of their oversize heads. The spine's tip glows in the murk of the anglerfish's habitat, acting as a natural fishing lure. When fish swim close to investigate, the anglerfish snaps them up in a mouth that can swallow prey twice her size. In other words, the anglerfish is a fish that fishes for other fish!

ORCHID MANTIS

WHERE THEY LIVE: FORESTS OF MALAYSIA

THEIR SECRET WEAPON: FLOWER POWER

The word "beautiful" isn't used often to describe a big bug, but the orchid mantis looks just like an awesome blossom. This alluring likeness is bad news for pollinating insects, which mistake the mantis's arms and legs for petals only to perish in its jaws when they buzz too close.

OWLS

WHERE THEY LIVE: NIGHT SKIES AROUND THE GLOBE

THEIR SECRET WEAPON: SNEAKY SOARING

With their keen vision adapted for hunting at night, powerful talons, and the ability in some species to swivel their heads nearly 300 degrees, owls are already unbeatable hunters. But they have one bonus ability that makes them the stealth fighters of hunting birds: silent flight. Feathers on the front edges of owl wings have a special serrated shape that reduces wind noise. And because their wings are so massive, owls don't have to flap as much as other birds. Their prey never hears them coming.

'STACHE'S SECRET

Although cone snail venom is one of nature's deadliest—and humans occasionally die from snail stings—researchers have been able to modify proteins in the toxin to create painkilling medications.

OUT OF SIGHT

The Many Kinds of Animal Camouflage

SHARKS HAVE IT. SO DO OWLS AND INSECTS, POLAR BEARS AND OCTOPUSES, FOXES AND FLOUNDERS. THEY'VE ALL EVOLVED WITH CAMOUFLAGE: physical characteristics that disguise their appearance to blend in with the background or otherwise fool other animals. Also known as "cryptic coloration," camouflage can take the form of striped fur, funky feathers, quick-changing skin, and other nifty natural disguises. It's what helps predators sneak up on prey and prey hide from predators. In the critter-eat-critter world of the wild, after all, animals that stand out sometimes end up as supper.

PERFECT BLENDS The most typical type of camouflage is "background matching," or blending into the environment. For example, polar bear fur matches the snow. A tiger's stripes blend with tall grass. Some animals change their look with the season. The arctic fox's fur shifts from brown to white in wintertime. And some camouflage has to be seen—or unseen—to be believed. Try to find the eastern screech owl on the opposite page.

'STACHE'S SECRET

You'd think a zebra's vibrant stripes would act like a neon sign advertising an easy meal. It turns out lions—the zebra's main predator—are color-blind. To them, the zebra's stripes look the same color as the background grasses.

MATCHING STRIPES Standing out from the crowd is a bad thing for animals that live in herds or schools, so they often sport camouflage that makes them blend with each other rather than the environment. A zebra's vibrant stripes serve two functions: They break up the animal's shape (a tactic known as "disruptive coloration") as well as match the fur of its herd neighbors, making it hard for a lion to see where one zebra ends and the next one begins.

COPYCATS Some animals are mimics, or clones of other animals or objects. A Southeast Asian insect called the walking leaf is a perfect example. Its body looks just like a tree leaf—right down to the simulated chomp marks from caterpillars. (It even sways while it walks to imitate a leaf blowing in the wind.) Some butterflies and moths, meanwhile, sport eyelike spots on their wings to fool predators into thinking they're scary owls.

COSTUME CHANGES Like a wizard out of the Harry Potter books, nature's all-stars of sneakiness can change their appearance in the blink of an eye. Octopuses, squids, and cuttlefish will alter their skin's color and texture to mimic rocks and morph into corals. Soft-bodied mollusks called nudibranchs rely on their diet to change colors—the brighter the better (poisonous animals often bear bright, colorful markings as a warning to predators).

BOTTOMS UP The tops and bottoms of "counter-colored animals" don't match. Sharks and penguins rely on such counter-shading to sneak through the sea unseen. A shark's belly is a lighter tone to match the day-lit surface of the water above, while its back is dark to blend in with the murk below.

FAKING BAD

THE MILK SNAKE
A harmless ground snake is a mimic of...

HARMLESS MIMICS THAT DRESS DANGEROUSLY

THE CORAL SNAKE
North America's most venomous snake.

Not all animal camouflage is for blending in. To avoid becoming lunch, some creatures copy the appearance of toxic-to-the-tummy animals that share their habitat. Predators mistake these mimics for the real thing and back off to avoid deadly bites or upset stomachs. Some mimics even take on the appearance of their main predators. (That would be like you dressing up as a killer whale to hide from sharks!) Here's a look at some cunningly colored clones . . .

THE ASH BORER
A harmless clear-winged moth is a mimic of...

A COMMON WASP
A flying insect with a nasty sting.

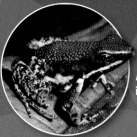

ALLOBATES ZAPARO FROG
A tasty but harmless frog in Ecuador is a mimic of...

EPIPEDOBATES PARVULUS FROG
A highly toxic member of the poison-dart-frog family. Do not eat!

THE HOVERFLY
A large, harmless fly that feeds on flower nectar is a mimic of...

A BEE AND WASP
Stinging insects that also buzz around flowers.

THE METALMARK MOTH
A helpless winged insect is a mimic of...

A JUMPING SPIDER
A common predator of the metalmark moth.

'STACHE'S SECRET

Remember this rhyme to tell the difference between a harmless milk snake and a deadly coral snake: "Red on yellow kills a fellow. Red on black is a friend of Jack." The rhyme's colorful words refer to the order of the snakes' stripes. If the snake has yellow stripes next to the red ones, keep your distance! (Actually, you probably shouldn't mess with a snake regardless of its color unless you are an experienced handler.)

TURN THE PAGE TO SEE THE MOST AMAZING MIMIC OF ALL!

MIGHTY MORPHING
MIMIC OCTOPUS!

MEET MOTHER NATURE'S MIGHTIEST MASTER OF DISGUISE

LOOK, IT'S A JELLYFISH! WAIT, NOW IT'S A STINGRAY! NO, IT'S
ACTUALLY A DEADLY SEA SNAKE! WATCHING THE INDO-MALAYAN
MIMIC OCTOPUS IS LIKE PLAYING SUBMARINE CHARADES. It can
imitate as many as 15 dangerous sea creatures! This master marine
impressionist has to keep up its act to survive. It's only two feet
(61 cm) long and completely harmless—a bite-size snack for a hungry
fish. But that same fish would think twice before nibbling on a poisonous
sea snake or spiny lionfish!

Like other "cephalopods" (octopus and cuttlefish), the mimic octopus is
covered with tiny color-shifting cells called chromatophores and is able
to change the texture of its skin. But while many cephalopods are known
to blend in with rocks and corals, only the mimic octopus copies the
behaviors and appearances of living creatures. Scientists credit the little
octopus's environment for these amazing powers of mimicry. It lurks
on the bottom of drab Indonesian river mouths that lack rocks or corals
to copy. Forced to hide in plain sight, the clever mimic imitates the next
best thing—its dangerous neighbors.

'STACHE'S SECRET
The mimic octopus isn't the ocean's only impressionist. When
threatened, the comet fish crams its face into a crevice and
makes its tail look like the head of a vicious moray eel.

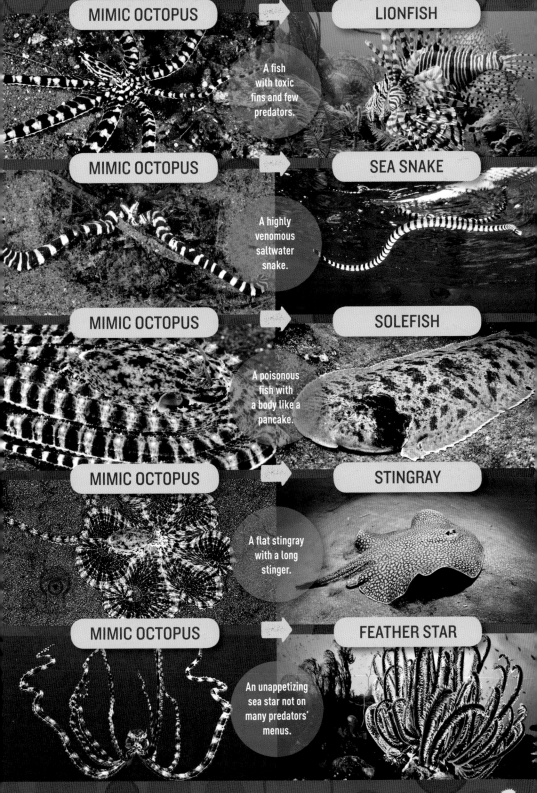

MIMIC OCTOPUS → LIONFISH

A fish with toxic fins and few predators.

MIMIC OCTOPUS → SEA SNAKE

A highly venomous saltwater snake.

MIMIC OCTOPUS → SOLEFISH

A poisonous fish with a body like a pancake.

MIMIC OCTOPUS → STINGRAY

A flat stingray with a long stinger.

MIMIC OCTOPUS → FEATHER STAR

An unappetizing sea star not on many predators' menus.

THE HIDDEN LIVES OF HOUSE CATS

UNDERCOVER KITTIES

YOUR CAT MIGHT LOOK CUTE WHEN SHE'S PURRING ON YOUR LAP, BUT LET HER OUT THE FRONT DOOR AND YOU'RE ACTUALLY UNLEASHING A BEAST! That's what researchers discovered when they strapped tiny National Geographic cameras to the collars of 60 house cats and let them roam the suburbs of Athens, Georgia, U.S.A. The cat's-eye footage revealed the disturbing secret lives of friendly felines. See for yourself, and you'll be ready to keep Fluffy indoors …

POWER PROWLERS Ever wish you could pet a panther? Stroking your cat is the next best thing. House cats share the same ancestor as lions, leopards, and other fearsome felines. They're like tiny tigers! And like tigers, kitties have killer instincts that never turn off. Nearly half of the cats in the camera-collar experiment stalked animals outdoors to supplement their bowl of Friskies back home. Lizards and small snakes topped the menu (when Mr. Whisker's whiskers stink, it's probably from lizard breath!), followed by chipmunks and birds—so many birds, in fact, that experts fear our feathered friends might be in danger of extinction in residential areas.

CRAWL-SPACE INVADERS Consider this the next time you let your tabby catnap on your pillow: He may have just crawled from the sewer! Cats are more flexible than dogs, able to squeeze through itty-bitty openings—a talent they use to pursue prey into storm drains, onto rooftops, and deep into the spider-infested crawl space under the house. It's true that house cats are famously fastidious, but remember: That tongue they use to groom does double duty as sandpaper to lick the fur from captured rodents.

HOUSE HUNTERS And now for the ultimate betrayal: At least one cat in the study lived a double life, splitting his time between two families who each thought they were the cat's true owners. The two-timing tabby would scratch at one house's door, nuzzle the owners, tuck into dinner, then scamper to the other house for a double dose of food and affection. So remember this the next time Fluffy purrs in your lap: You might not be the only human in her life!

GROSS ENCOUNTERS House cats in the kitty-cam study kept strange company, carousing with rats, stray dogs, and even opossums—all potentially aggressive animals and carriers of deadly rabies. A quarter of the cats also drank from puddles and other possibly poisonous sources of water. See, curiosity really can kill the cat!

THREE TIPS
FOR PROTECTING
TINY TIGERS

1.
Keep cats—especially young male cats—indoors as much as possible to protect both your kitty and the local bird population.

2.
Get your cat vaccinated against diseases spread by other animals.

3.
If you feel bad about keeping kitty cooped up, consider building an enclosed area outdoors.

HUSH PUPPY
THE SECRET LIFE
OF SPOT

COUNTER-SURFING: All good dogs know that kitchen counters are off limits—when you're home. You better believe they're scouring every surface for missed morsels as soon as you step out.

POOPER SCOOPERS: Some dogs turn the litter box into a buffet when you're not around. Poop-snacking pooches might have a diet lacking certain vitamins and digestion-aiding enzymes—enzymes they can get from caca.

ROLLING ROVER: It's bad enough when your dog digs up the yard, but … sniff, sniff? What's that foul smell? Fido's been frolicking in filth again! Some experts believe dogs instinctively roll in poop or dead critters to share these foul finds with pack members. Unfortunately in this case, you're part of your dog's pack!

23

Fab CRAB

SOMEWHERE OFF THE COAST OF SOUTH AFRICA, A TOOTHED CRAB IS DECIDING WHAT TO WEAR. It plucks a clump of seaweed, shredding it with sharp claws before sticking it to the Velcro-like surface of its shell. Presto! A seaweed shawl! Now to accessorize. A few bits of bright coral for the claws. Perhaps some anemone tentacles up on top. And to finish the ensemble, a flip-flop that floated from the mainland. Voîla! This crab is dressed for survival!

The toothed crab belongs to a large group of crustaceans known as decorator crabs, which live all over the world. While other animals rely on their fur, scales, feathers, or skin to camouflage their bodies, decorator crabs design their own camouflage from objects in their environment. They'll use any material that helps them blend in: plants, sponges, rocks, shells, corals, driftwood, and even bits of castaway human trash such as torn T-shirts, tires, and soggy sneakers.

When predators approach, the junk-covered crab freezes in place—just another bit of coral or rock or random piece of garbage. Some decorator crabs even cover themselves in poisonous seaweed or anemone tentacles. Predators that swim too close get shell-shocked!

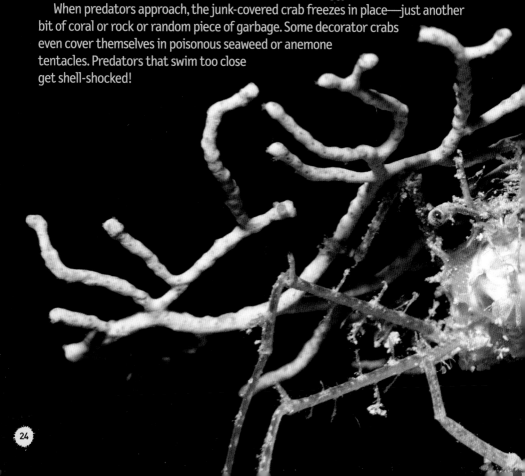

THE DECORATOR CRAB IS ONE SNAPPY—AND SNEAKY—DRESSER

CRAB *Couture*

When researchers placed a decorator crab in an aquarium full of trinkets, it dressed up in pearls and lace scavenged from the bottom. These crabs might have a horrible fashion sense—they've been known to mix solids with stripes and wear white after Labor Day—but then it's not like they're dressing up for dinner. They're dressing to avoid becoming dinner.

DODGING JAWS

Could shark-spoofing wet suits keep surfers from getting chomped?

Shark bites on people are extremely rare (you're more likely to get struck by lightning), but surfers and swimmers still feel like bait when they bob in the waters off notoriously "sharky" beaches. If mimicry and camouflage can help animals outwit predators, shouldn't the same tactics protect people when they're not on top of the food chain? That's the theory behind wet suit technology from Shark Attack Mitigation Systems, a company based in Perth, Australia. A rise in fatal attacks along the Western Australian coastline—a hunting ground for great white sharks—prompted research into anti-chomp strategies. The result: wet suits designed to make surfers, divers, and snorkelers "invisible" to sharks, or at least appear unappetizing.

The suits' designers studied shark eyesight to figure out just how these powerful sea predators see their prey. Turns out many of the more dangerous sharks are color-blind, and the designers used this knowledge to create a "cryptic" wet suit meant to camouflage humans so they can swim with the fishes without ending up sleeping with the fishes. For surfers, the designers created a vibrantly striped "warning" pattern that mimics the appearance of poisonous marine creatures that sharks avoid.

Of course, the wet suits only interfere with a shark's sight. These fish rely on many other senses to detect prey, including smell, taste, hearing, and even the ability to sense electrical signals given off by living creatures. The bold stripes of the warning suit might even attract sharks rather than repel them, according to one shark expert. "Sharks see contrast particularly well," says George Burgess, director of the Florida Program for Shark Research. "Patterns that stick out may be more attractive. My choice would be to go for blending in rather than sticking out." If nothing else, the fancy suits might provide surfers and divers with the peace of mind they don't get from standard wet suits, which tend to "disguise" humans as sleek seals and sea lions—a great white's favorite meals.

BITER BEWARE

Beach bathers who don't have the budget for a $495 shark-deterring wet suit can buy a much cheaper rash guard that mimics the stripes of a poisonous lionfish.

"WARNING" WET SUIT

Bold stripes on the sleeves and legs of the surfing wet suit bring to mind an escaped prisoner rather than a pro surfer, but this fashion statement serves a purpose: The stripes mimic the coloration of dangerous marine creatures, such as sea snakes and lionfish, which sharks avoid. The pattern is also available as a sticker for surfboards and scuba tanks.

"CRYPTIC" WET SUIT

Designed for scuba divers and people who spearfish, this suit features a more muted design that blends into the deep blue of the ocean background. Field tests showed that tiger sharks ignored bait wrapped in this pattern but gladly chomped on regular suits stuffed with fish.

IT'S A TRAP!

We head down the hatch of the world's sneakiest spider

Knock knock. CHOMP! Ask a trap-door spider for a knock-knock joke and you won't laugh at the punch line—especially if you're an itty-bitty bug or a tiny rodent (the spider's favorite snacks). This group of medium-size spiders—which includes roughly 120 species spread across the world—is famous for its horrible hospitality.

Each trap-door spider digs an underground burrow (although some prefer to live in trees) complete with a small door made of leaves, algae, and dirt, which blends in with the surrounding soil. It even has a tiny hinge fashioned from a squirt of spider silk. Outside the hatch, the spider weaves its "welcome mat": a network of silk strands that all lead back to the burrow. Once construction is done, the spider "locks" its door by holding it shut with barbed fangs. Then it hunkers down and waits for company.

As darkness falls, a hapless beetle scurries toward the nocturnal spider's hidey-hole, stumbling across the silken trip wires leading to the hatch. Vibrations in the strands mean one thing: Company's coming! The spider waits for the beetle to creep closer and closer until it's right outside the door. Then—woosh! In the blink of an eye, the trap-door spider opens the hatch and pulls in the tasty beetle. And that's why you'd never want to drop by a trap-door spider's house uninvited.

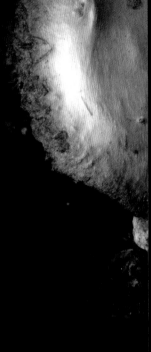

28

More Sneaky Spiders

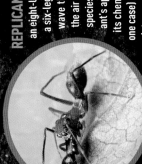

SILK STALKING While most spiders weave webbing only from their abdomens (aka, their backsides), so-called "spitting spiders" can actually shoot twin streams of sticky, venom-smeared silk from their mouths. These sharpshooters take aim from up to an inch (2.5 cm) away before delivering a double-barreled blast of silk to incapacitate prey.

REPLICANT ANT How can an eight-legged spider imitate a six-legged ant? Easy: They wave their front legs in the air like antenna. Many species of spiders copy the ant's appearance (and even its chemical signature, in one case) as protection from predators, which avoid eating bitter-tasting ants. Some spider disguises are so effective they even fool real ants, which stand by while the mimics march through their colony to devour defenseless members.

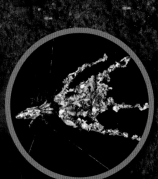

PUPPET MASTER When researchers came across a one-inch (2.5-cm)-high eight-legged form squirming in a web in the Peruvian rain forest, they thought they'd found a new species of spider. A closer inspection revealed that the arachnid was actually just bits of dead bugs, debris, and leaves, all carefully smashed together and shaken to life by a smaller spider living in the same web. The little spider had constructed the larger decoy of itself to scare away birds and other predators.

DOUBLE-CROSSER: Predators can't make heads or tails of the African two-headed snake, which has a tail that looks like its head and a head that looks like its tail. Its phony head "watches" from atop its coiled body while the real head slithers through nearby underbrush to hunt. Completing the illusion, the counterfeit head whips around in mock strikes as the snake retreats.

BEST ACTOR: The piping plover deserves a parent-of-the-year award, or at least an Academy Award. When a predator threatens its nest, the little shorebird flops around like it has a broken wing to trick the trespasser into following along. Once the predator has been lured safely away, this natural-born actor straightens its wing, takes a bow, and flies back to the nest (okay, we made up the part about the bow).

ODOR EATER: Stinkiness is the key to survival for the California ground squirrel. It chews the shed skin of its main predator—the rattlesnake—into a sticky paste, which it smears all over its fluffy tail. Rattlesnakes avoid the smelly squirrel for fear of attacking one of their own kind.

CREATURE Cunning

SUPREMELY SNEAKY — Trap-Door Spider

DEFINITELY DEVIOUS — Leopard

Mimic Octopus

SOLIDLY STEALTHY — Decorator Crab

SLIGHTLY SHIFTY — Cone Snail

Spitting Spider

SHHH SCALE

SPECTRUM OF HUSH-HUSH HIERARCHY

Secret Agent 'Stache
Ranks **WILY WILDLIFE**

CHAPTER 2

Seeing Isn't Believing

REALITY IS A RARITY THESE DAYS.

Artists use computers to create convincing worlds and creatures that fool the eye. Photographers "touch up" celebrity photos to erase pimples and wrinkles. Advertisers and hoaxers upload phony stories hoping they'll go "viral"—shared by millions on the Internet. Even "reality" television shows hire writers and follow scripts. From food photos that fool you to computer-generated deceptions, this chapter exposes the many ways marketers, artists, and everyday tricksters try to pass off the unreal as real. By the time you finish reading, you won't believe your eyes.

PHONY FEAST

The tasty-looking tricks of **food photographers** . . .

IT'S A DINNER THAT WOULD MAKE MOST PEOPLE DROOL.
Plump, juicy chicken. Fresh veggies seared on the grill. A steaming spud smothered in butter. Strawberries dipped in vanilla ice cream for dessert. And to wash it all down, a tall glass of icy milk. But before you take that first bite, beware! That chicken is half raw and stuffed with paper towels. Those strawberries are colored with lipstick. And don't even think of drinking the milk—unless you like the taste of dish soap!

This dinner isn't for dining on. It's been carefully prepared and arranged—down to the bubbles in the beverage—for a photo shoot. "Food stylists" rely on all sorts of tricks to make meals and dishes look scrumptious for commercials, cookbooks, and restaurant menus. "Styling has become more natural looking in the past 20 years," says Lisa Cherkasky, a food stylist for more than two decades, "but don't think those crumbs and drips you see in ads were not thought about and styled carefully!" Here's what's on the menu of a typical souped-up supper . . .

SPOILER ALERT
THIS FOOD WON'T SPOIL!

GAG BAG

The "Anti-Theft Lunch Bag" works like a food stylist in reverse. It disguises your sandwich as a moldy mess! The mold is actually a pattern painted on each plastic sandwich bag (a pack of 25 bags costs $8), but potential lunch looters won't know that!

MAGIC MILK

Stylists often substitute kindergarten glue for milk in photos of cereal so the flakes don't get soggy. Dish soap is dabbled on the surface of many drinks to give that fresh-poured look.

THE PERFECT BIRD

This chicken is half-baked, stuffed with napkins, and painted with food coloring to make it look juicy. Cherkasky has an easy fix for any rips in raw meat: superglue!

SOUR CREAM

Real ice cream would melt into gooey soup under the studio's hot lights, so stylists simulate fresh scoops using cake icing and powdered sugar. Dull strawberries go to the makeup chair for a lipstick touch-up.

BAD BREAD

To keep bread from drying out, stylists spritz it with a waterproofing spray designed to protect car dashboards. Um, yum! "I rarely get hungry for the food I'm styling," says Cherkasky.

NOT-HOT POTATO

In all likelihood, this spud sat around in the studio for hours waiting for its close-up. To duplicate that freshly cooked look, the stylist microwaves a soggy cotton ball and hides it behind food to create steam.

UNREAL GRILL

Cherkasky uses a burnt matchstick to draw those perfect char marks on veggies, burgers, chicken—anything that needs to look fresh from the flame. Eyeliner also does the trick.

THE HALL *of* TALL TALES

Hoaxes Throughout History

1593

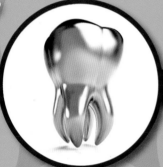

1869

GIANT LIE

A ten-foot (3-m)-tall stone man uncovered by workers digging a well becomes an instant tourist attraction in Cardiff, New York, U.S.A., luring thousands of visitors who pay up to 50 cents to see the rock colossus. Debate rages over whether the giant is a petrified man from biblical times or a century-old statue created to impress the locals. Truth be told, the "Cardiff Giant" is actually a sculpture commissioned by a tobacco grower and buried as a prank. Its "discovery" was no accident, either, and the prankster earns a small fortune from all of the hubbub. The giant is such a crowd-pleaser, in fact, that circus showman P. T. Barnum copies it. He's later taken to court in a case that reveals the truth behind both bogus giants.

TRUTH DECAY

A boy with a golden tooth becomes the talk of central Europe and the focus of intense medical study. After checking out the precious chopper, a professor proclaims it is genuine, perhaps the result of a curious alignment of planets during the boy's birth. As the gilded molar begins to break down from daily wear, the boy refuses to let anyone inspect it. Soon, the truth of the tooth is revealed: It's a golden cap fitted over an existing tooth—the first of its type.

'STACHE'S SECRET

Sometimes "hoaxes" turn out to be real. When naturalists in the early 1800s saw the first preserved platypus specimens, they thought the duck-billed creatures were fakes stitched together from other animals. Nope! Today we know these odd egg-laying mammals really exist!

1938

MARS ATTACKS

Radio listeners tuning in to a Halloween broadcast of H. G. Wells's science-fiction book *The War of the Worlds* believe it's a genuine news report of a Martian invasion. The program isn't intended as a hoax—it actually contains two disclaimers that it's a work of fiction—but some listeners still panic..

1991

CROCK CIRCLES

When intricate swirls started appearing in English cornfields in the 1970s, believers in the paranormal hailed them as evidence of artistic visitors from outer space. Crop-circle fever gripped the nation—until two pranksters in 1991 admit they used ropes and boards to press at least some of the mysterious designs into the fields.

1994

SNEAKY SERPENT

A London surgeon supposedly photographed the slender neck of "Nessie" poking from Scotland's Loch Ness in 1934, and the photo became the longest-standing piece of photographic proof that a serpent lurks in the lake. Sixty years later, a person involved with the picture admits it's a hoax—just a plastic model glued to a tin toy submarine.

1917

FAIRY FAIL

A pair of mischievous girls in Cottingley, England, pose in photos with cardboard cutouts of fairies clipped from a children's book. The pictures become a sensation across England, even fooling Sherlock Holmes creator Sir Arthur Conan Doyle. The girls admit to the hoax much later in life.

2009

UFO NO!

News helicopters scramble to pursue a silver saucer-shaped balloon adrift in the Colorado, U.S.A., sky after amateur inventor Richard Heene reports that his six-year-old son, Falcon, is inside the makeshift UFO. When police find the craft crashed and empty near the Denver airport, they fear that young Falcon had fallen. Fortunately, the boy is safe at home, hiding in the attic. The entire incident was an elaborate hoax plotted by Falcon's parents to land a reality TV show.

2007

iPHONY SCIENCE

A website popular for offering household advice posts a video showing how to charge an iPod using an onion and Gatorade. Millions watch the video—and several websites report it as fact—but unsuccessful efforts to duplicate the experiment show it to be a hoax. The site soon earns a reputation for posting phony "life hacks."

FALSE TEETH

FOSSIL HUNTERS FLOCK TO
SOUTHERN ENGLAND'S "JURASSIC
COAST" TO COMB ITS ROCKY
BEACHES FOR THE PETRIFIED
BONES OF PREHISTORIC BEASTS,
but what they found one morning in
summer 2013 could have rewritten
natural history. Here, emerging from
the sand from the backbone up, sat a
fearsome skull the size of a minivan.
Gnarled horns sprouted from atop its
ridged head. Its mouth sported fangs
nearly as tall as the curious beach-
combers strolling nearby.

The locals were accustomed
to discovering fossils of
ichthyosaurs and other
ancient aquatic

creatures on Jurassic Coast beaches,
but this was something else entirely.
It appeared to belong to a dragon.

Instead of bone, however, the skull
was made of Styrofoam. It was a fake!
Three artists spent more than a month
designing, building, and painting the
phony bones. They hauled it onto the
beach before dawn and left it for early
risers to discover. Word of the dragon

HOW **BOGUS** DRAGON BONES ENDED UP ON AN ENGLISH BEACH

traveled fast across the Internet. Which was precisely the intention of its creators. The skull was a piece of "viral marketing"—an attempt to build buzz by tricking people into talking about it online. The project was the brainchild of an advertising agency paid to promote a new fantasy television show featuring dragons. The agency issued a press release timed with the skull's "discovery," ensuring that every website covering the Jurassic Coast dragon would also mention the television show. So the next time you see something stupendous, think twice before hyping it online. You're probably just giving someone free advertising.

WEB *of* DECEIT

THREE INTERNET SENSATIONS THAT WERE SECRETLY ADS

FLOATING FEET

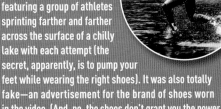

Millions of web surfers fell for an online video demonstrating the art of "liquid mountaineering," aka running on water. The footage looked legit, featuring a group of athletes sprinting farther and farther across the surface of a chilly lake with each attempt (the secret, apparently, is to pump your feet while wearing the right shoes). It was also totally fake—an advertisement for the brand of shoes worn in the video. (And, no, the shoes don't grant you the power of liquid mountaineering.)

THE JAYWALKING DEAD

Talk about a rotten trick. When photos surfaced online showing hordes of zombies shambling through the streets of New York City, U.S.A., people wondered if an undead outbreak was at hand. They had nothing to fear. The "zombies" were actually actors in makeup. An ad agency unleashed them in the city to promote a TV show about the walking dead.

POPBOT

Billed as "the world's first fully automated, voice-activated popcorn shooter" on its website, the Popinator robot launched pieces of popcorn straight into the mouth of anyone who said the word "pop." It looked like the greatest snack-based invention since the Sno-Kone machine, but unfortunately the Popinator was a phony prototype created to promote a popcorn company.

LIES, CAMERA,

FIVE WAYS
MOVIES
FOOL THE EYE

MOVIE DIRECTORS ARE MASTERS OF MAKE-BELIEVE—BUT ONLY IF YOU ACTUALLY BELIEVE IN THE WORLDS AND CHARACTERS THEY MAKE. That's why they hire armies of "effects artists" who toil behind the scenes to bring supernatural creatures or spaceship battles from script to screen. Here's a look at the most effective special effects from the history of sneaky cinema ...

GREEN SCREEN Similar to the matte-painting technique (except much more sophisticated), a green-screen effect places the actors into any environment the director wishes. The actors don't actually see the setting, though. They stand in front of a huge green screen—sometimes the entire soundstage is green—and pretend to react to creatures and environmental effects that replace the green background later. It takes some imagination on the actors' parts to react to things they can't see at the time of filming, but that's why they call it acting!
As seen in: The more recent Star Wars films were filmed almost entirely on green-screen sets. In many cases, the actors didn't know what their characters were seeing until the movie was finished!

MAKEUP Movie makeup effects go way beyond the application of foundation or eye shadow to doll up the actors. Hollywood makeup artists use all sorts of tricks and special materials—from latex skin to artificial body parts—to make actors look old, injured, or like they just landed from another planet.
As seen in: Harry Potter and the Goblet of Fire. Makeup effects turned actor Brendan Gleeson into the heavily scarred, eyesight-challenged "Mad-Eye" Moody.

ACTION!

MATTE PAINTINGS You've seen this simple illusion in a million movies and TV shows. It starts when a "matte artist" paints a realistic-looking backdrop—an alien landscape or strange building, for instance—on a large piece of glass, which is then placed in front of the camera. When the actors are filmed through the unpainted portion of the glass, it appears as if they're actually in the environment of the painting. The best matte artists create scenes that look completely real, but the process has fallen out of style now that computer-graphics artists can create environments that move and come alive around the actors.
As seen in: Raiders of the Lost Ark. *The endless warehouse where the ark is stored at the end of the film is actually a matte painting.*

STOP-MOTION ANIMATION One of the oldest special effects also takes the most patience to put together. Effects artists first create a highly poseable miniature model of a creature or vehicle. They pose the model, snap a picture, make a tiny adjustment to the model's pose, snap another picture, and on, and on. Hours later, when they play the photo frames in a rapid sequence, it appears as if the models are moving with a life of their own.
As seen in: Jason and the Argonauts. *Effects wizard Ray Harryhausen—a pioneer in stop-motion animation—brought mobs of scary skeletons to life in this classic romp through Greek mythology.*

MINIATURES When effects artists need to portray something big—a futuristic city, medieval castle, or supersize spaceship—they build small. Modelmakers painstakingly piece together realistic and detailed miniature places and spaces, which are then filmed from a perspective that makes them look life-size—or larger. Destroying these scale cities and structures (say, for a monster movie) is much easier and cheaper than demolishing a real-life metropolis!
As seen in: The Lord of the Rings movies, which *featured scale models for their fantastical castles and fortresses. Perspective tricks also made normal-size actors look like pint-size hobbits.*

TURN THE PAGE TO SEE THE MOST AMAZING SPECIAL EFFECTS OF ALL! ➡

Digital
DECEPTION

Computer-generated imagery completes the illusion

IT LOOKED LIKE A TYPICAL AMATEUR WILDLIFE VIDEO—JUST JITTERY FOOTAGE OF AN EXTRA-LARGE EAGLE GLIDING ABOVE A CANADIAN PUBLIC PARK. THEN SOMETHING AMAZING HAPPENED. The eagle banked, dove, and dug its talons into a toddler sitting in the grass beside his dad. The bird seemed on the verge of whisking the boy to some unknown fate. Then, miraculously, it released the toddler unhurt.

The 30-second video—uploaded to video-sharing websites under the name "Golden Eagle Snatches Kid"—became an instant viral hit, passed around via email and viewed by more than two million people in 48 hours. Wildlife experts speculated about the eagle's behavior. Artists scrutinized the video for signs that it was phony. Wary parents scanned the skies for vicious birds of prey.

They needn't have worried. The bird was bogus—a three-dimensional (3-D) model created and animated with a computer program. Even the toddler was entirely digital. The 30-second clip was created by third-year students at the Centre NAD, an animation school in Montreal, Canada. Instead of getting a scolding for fooling people with their project, the students received a perfect grade! Their assignment had been to create a hoax video with the potential to go viral.

The stunt had been an exercise in creating realistic computer-generated imagery (CGI): the same special-effects technology used to bring dinosaurs to life and make Harry Potter grab the golden snitch on movie screens. Such effects have come a long way in just 15 years, thanks to a huge leap in computing power. "If we were to ask a machine from 1993 to render an image created today, the time required to do so would be prohibitive," says Robin Tremblay, professor of visual effects at Centre NAD.

Today, digital artists can create convincing animals, monsters, cities, and objects, but one species of creature still presents a challenge: humans. Because we see flesh-and-blood people on a daily basis, we're especially good at noticing the slightest imperfections in computer-generated people. And while CGI technology continues to improve, so does our ability to detect it—hence the immediate skepticism of the kid-snatching eagle. "We get used to seeing digital effects," says Tremblay. "The quest for 100 percent realistic CG shots continues!"

RENDERING LIFE:
CGI IN THREE STEPS

Step 1) CG characters start as a basic model called a render, which is assembled from 3-D shapes called polygons.

Step 2) Textures are digitally "painted" on the model to give it details: skin, scales, facial features, buttons, tattoos, etc.

Step 3) The textured model is inserted into a real or virtual environment. Artists add virtual light sources that reflect on the surfaces of the model, making it look like a natural part of the scene. "The main breakthrough that allowed CGI to become much more realistic is lighting," Tremblay says.

SEEING

SUBLIMINAL ADVERTISING
AND SECRET IMAGES

RESEARCHER JAMES VICARY POPULARIZED THE CONCEPT OF "SUBLIMINAL ADVERTISING"—SUPPOSED HIDDEN MESSAGES THAT ONLY THE SUBCONSCIOUS CAN DETECT—IN 1957, WHEN HE INSERTED THE WORDS "DRINK COCA-COLA" AND "EAT POPCORN" INTO A MOVIE CALLED *PICNIC*. The words flashed on the screen for just a fraction of a second—too fast for the eye to detect—but Vicary proclaimed that sales of popcorn and Coke jumped among viewers. His results were later debunked, and more recent studies show that subliminal messaging doesn't work, but that hasn't stopped advertisers from hiding words and images for your mind's eye. (Try to) see for yourself ...

FLAVOR SAVER
Baskin Robbins' logo serves two purposes: It showcases the name of the ice cream and advertises its 31 flavors. Can you spot the number?

WINNING GRIN
The smile in the Amazon logo is obvious, but look again and you'll see that it hypes the online store's large selection: everything from A to Z.

THINGS

MITT WIT
The Milwaukee Brewers' initials are built right into the team's old logo.

DOUBLE DIPPERS
Scrutinize the Tostitos logo to spot two people splitting a chip over a bowl of salsa.

ANIMAL HOUSE
The logo for the Pittsburgh Zoo is a real jungle. How many creatures do you see hidden in the tree?

BARELY THERE BEAR
The Matterhorn mountain beside the logo of Swiss candy-bar company Toblerone is easy to see, but peek inside the peak and you'll spot a bear—a symbol of the chocolate factory's home city.

SAWED IN HALF...
SOLVED!

Revealing the Secret Behind a Classic Magic Trick

You've probably seen this scenario played out in dozens of magic shows: The magician locks his or her assistant into a coffin-like enclosure before proceeding to saw the box in two. Slicing implements vary, but the result is always the same: The assistant spends a few seconds neatly halved before emerging in one piece, smiling and unhurt, from the reassembled box. Thrilling? Certainly, but this famous illusion is a triumph of sneakiness rather than magic. See the saw trick from the inside out in this by-the-second breakdown...

Dissecting the Saw Trick

0:01 The magician swaggers onstage to present his or her assistant.

0:17 Out rolls the magic box on wheels. The assistant spins the box for the audience's inspection.

0:20 Go time! The magician undoes the latches on the box and opens its two top doors. The assistant climbs inside, placing his or her head, hands, and feet through holes. The magician slaps the doors shut and locks the latches.

1:03 Let's sneak a peek inside the box. While the magician distracts the audience by readying the saw, the assistant—typically a skilled contortionist—draws his or her legs to the top half of the box. Those feet wriggling from the holes at the other end? They're fake.

1:18 With a dramatic flourish, the magician thrusts the cutting tool through the box, neatly slicing it in two. The bottom and top halves are pulled apart as the assistant's head, hands, and (robotic) feet wriggle.

1:39 The magician connects the two halves and removes the blade. Inside, the relieved assistant stretches his or her legs to the bottom of the box.

1:45 Just before the magician undoes the latches and opens the box, the assistant pulls the robot feet back inside along with his or her head and hands. Up comes the lid and out springs the smiling assistant, in one piece and ready for the next trick. Cue audience applause.

SPELL CHECK
MORE ILLUSIONS SOLVED

STANDING LEVITATION

Using nothing but the power of his or her mind, a magician straightens up and rises slightly off the ground (but he or she is secretly standing on tiptoe in one shoe while keeping the sole of that shoe on the ground).

HORIZONTAL LEVITATION

The magician lays an assistant on his or her back, then—presto! The assistant appears to hover in the air in front of the magician (but the assistant is actually held aloft by a support disguised as the magician's leg).

BULLET-CATCHING TRICK

Staring death in the face, a magician stands before a gun-wielding assistant. The assistant fires the gun and—gasp!—the magician smiles to reveal the bullet caught in his or her teeth (but the gun fired a blank, and the magician had squirreled away a fake bullet in his or her mouth).

SNEAKY Snap

PHOTOS THAT FOOL YOU

BOGUS GHOST

To promote his magic show, illusionist Henri Robin used double exposure—a technique that combines two photos—to create this haunting image in 1863.

A PICTURE'S WORTH A THOUSAND WORDS, THE OLD SAYING GOES, BUT NOT ALL OF THOSE WORDS ARE NECESSARILY TRUE. Ever since the invention of the camera, photographers have been figuring out ways to retouch, airbrush, double-expose, and otherwise "doctor" their images. And today's digital cameras—which upload their contents directly to computers— make it easier than ever to fiddle with photos using powerful programs. Detecting deceptive imagery is nearly impossible for untrained eyes, so we've rounded up some famous examples to reveal the trickery behind them ...

SHOOTING STARS

Movie stars and pop icons spend a fortune to look forever young, fit, and glamorous, so you better believe they're picky about their pictures on magazine covers and in advertisements. Art directors break out all their digital tricks to "airbrush" pimples, wrinkles, flabby bits, and other imperfections from the celebrities' faces and bodies. Don't feel left out! School photographers use similar techniques to give high school students the star treatment in yearbook pics.

shots

HORSE PLAY

Pics of politicians and powerful leaders are often manipulated to make them look more heroic. In this 1942 photo of Italian prime minister Benito Mussolini, the image of his horse handler was erased—a painstaking process of retouching by hand in the days before computerized photo manipulation.

Forty years earlier, U.S. president and Civil War general Ulysses S. Grant became the subject of a dashing picture on horseback created from three separate images.

HEAD GAMES

Next time your yearbook photo makes you cringe, consider this: Nobody looks perfect all the time. Not even celebrities. On a 1989 *TV Guide* cover, art directors decided on a last minute swap and put Oprah's head on a picture of 1960s movie star Ann-Margret's body in a glamorous sequin dress. But this was hardly the first noggin transplant in history. In a portrait dated from roughly 1860, the head of U.S. president Abraham Lincoln was grafted onto the body of John Calhoun—a southern politician who had actually died ten years earlier. Lincoln's photographers preferred Calhoun's regal pose, even though Calhoun's beliefs stood in sharp contrast to Lincoln's.

SHOP TALK

When it was released in 1990, the computer program Photoshop ushered in a new age of photo tomfoolery. Suddenly any amateur photographer with a PC or Mac could fiddle with pictures—from simple retouching to creating elaborate, otherworldly vistas. The shocking shark scene above, which made the rounds on the Internet under the guise of "National Geographic's Photo of the Year," is a classic example. It was actually a clever composite shot created by digitally combining photos of a helicopter hovering over the San Francisco Bay with a breaching great white shark from South Africa.

ARTISTIC LICENSE

Not all doctored photos are created to deceive. Swedish photographer Erik Johansson layers dozens—sometimes hundreds—of pictures to create elaborate illusions that look both real and surreal.

'STACHE'S SECRET

Photoshop has become such a commonly used tool for manipulating photos that its nickname is now a verb. When web surfers come across any of the many questionable photos on the Internet, they debate whether the photos are real or 'shopped.

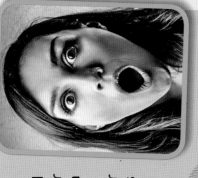

SURPRISE PARTIES: Every good surprise party begins with a small deception for the birthday girl or boy—a trip around the block, an invitation to a movie that never materializes, or any number of other well-timed distractions from what's really the main event: a crowd of accomplices meeting in the dark waiting to yell "surprise!"

FLASH MOBS: A flash mob happens when a group of practical jokesters meet in a public place, put on an elaborate—and seemingly spontaneous—performance, then beat a hasty retreat. Flash mobsters organize all sorts of silly activities: pillow fights, choreographed dances, reenacted movie scenes—even four minutes spent frozen in place.

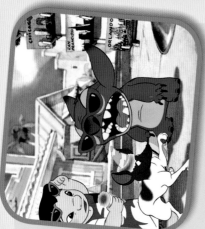

EASTER EGGS: Ever since a programmer named Warren Robinett hid his initials in the Atari video game *Adventure* in 1979, game designers and moviemakers have been hiding characters, images, and messages in the their creations for viewers to find. (Can you spot the Disney World postcard in the scene from *Lilo & Stitch* shown above?) The sneaky idea behind these "Easter eggs" isn't a new one. Italian researchers probing the peepers of the "Mona Lisa," Leonardo DaVinci's famous painting, noticed the letters "LV" in her right eye (perhaps the artist's initials) and some indecipherable symbols in her left. It's not just the Mona Lisa's smile that's mysterious!

ALTERED
Realities

SHHH SCALE

SPECTRUM OF HUSH-HUSH HIERARCHY

Secret Agent 'Stache Ranks Attempts at **TRICKERY**

SUPREMELY SNEAKY	Doctored Photos
DEFINITELY DEVIOUS	Subliminal Advertising
SOLIDLY STEALTHY	Computer-Generated Imagery
SLIGHTLY SHIFTY	Viral Marketing
	Food Photography

CHAPTER 3

Sneaks, Cheats, and Scoundrels

IT'S NOT EASY BEING SNEAKY.

SERIOUSLY! A 2012 Tufts University study showed that sneakiness can suck the life out of you. People who kept big secrets complained that even little tasks were tougher. Groceries felt heavier. Walking the dog was a chore. Hills seemed steeper. But for some natural-born sneaks, bearing a secret burden doesn't weigh them down—it's a way of life! Prepare to enter the sneaky world of con artists, cyber crooks, masters of disguise, and other professional fibbers who are good at being bad.

BRIDGE *for* SALE

GEORGE C. PARKER HAD AN OFFER YOU COULDN'T REFUSE IN THE EARLY 1900s—ESPE- CIALLY IF YOU WERE A NEW ARRIVAL IN THE "LAND OF OPPORTUNITY." Parker gained fame for approaching tourists and immigrants in New York City and selling them some of the city's most amazing landmarks. The Brooklyn Bridge, the Statue of Liberty, Grant's Tomb, the Metro- politan Museum of Art—all were up for sale, and Parker found plenty of buyers.

It was all a con—a moneymaking scheme also known as a scam, flimflam, sham, swindle, hustle, grift, bamboozle, or confidence trick—and Parker was a legendary "confidence man." He forged documents and worked from a phony office to gain the trust of his victims (called "marks"). For years, Parker's bamboozling business boomed. Some weeks he managed to sell the Brooklyn Bridge twice!

Parker wasn't the only flimflam man peddling prime NYC real estate at the turn of the century. Selling the Brooklyn Bridge was a popular sham. Brothers Charles and Fred Gondorf would often prop up a "Bridge For Sale" sign when police weren't looking and unload the landmark on the first sucker who strolled

HUSTLE UP

BAIT AND SWITCH

This old sales trick lures customers with an insanely low price for a particular product. The clerk then explains that the advertised item is out of stock, then pressures the customer to buy a "better," more expensive replacement.

PONZI SCHEME

Pioneered by Italian businessman and con artist Charles Ponzi, this financial scam hoodwinks investors by paying them money swindled from new investors rather than actual investments. Eventually the scheme unravels and the mastermind runs off with everyone's money.

THREE-CARD MONTE

The swindler places three cards—a queen and two random ones—on the table faceup for the mark's inspection, then flips the cards over and shuffles their order. The mark wins if he or she can find the "lady," but the con artist uses sleight of hand to make sure the queen never gets picked.

along. The price ranged from a thousand bucks to just $250, depending on how much cash the mark carried.

How could anyone fall for such an obvious scam? Greed was one reason. Confidence men convinced marks they could make big bucks by charging tolls and admission prices on their famous properties. (The marks realized they'd been swindled when police arrived to remove their makeshift tollbooths.) The most cunning con men bribed the crew of international vessels for info on well-to-do passengers keen on acquiring real estate. And remember: These cons happened long before TV or the Internet. Many immigrants arrived naive and eager to buy their slice of the U.S.A.

Eventually, the marks grew savvy and the con artists got caught. Parker was sentenced to life in New York's Sing Sing Prison in 1928 for his many swindles. The sale of the Brooklyn Bridge lives on as the ultimate bamboozle. Today's swindlers have moved into new territory—the Internet—where they've found new bridges to sell.

OUT *of* TUNE

Milli Vanilli's Musical Masquerade

FAB MORVAN AND ROB PILATUS WERE POP STARS ON TOP OF THE WORLD IN 1989. The two former models from Germany had been signed as the singers of Milli Vanilli, a funky, hip-hop dance act whose debut American album was crammed with chart-topping hits. They even won a Grammy Award for Best New Artist. Then the music died—literally.

The duo was performing their most well-known hit, a catchy tune called "Girl You Know It's True," live on MTV when the song began stuttering, repeating the lyric "girl you know it's…" Suddenly revealed as lip-synchers—performers pretending to sing—the flummoxed Morvan and Pilatus bolted from the stage.

Lip-synching isn't uncommon in live performances. Artists who dance on stage often move their mouth to a prerecorded track so they don't sound breathless and out of tune as they boogie. But Morvan and Pilatus's technical glitch was just another sign that something fishy was going on with Milli Vanilli. Music executives wondered how two men from Germany had managed to record an album with perfect American accents. Then a performer came forward claiming he was one of the three singers behind Milli Vanilli's songs—and that Morvan and Pilatus were not the other two.

Producer Frank Farian admitted that Morvan's and Pilatus's voices weren't on the album. Milli Vanilli had been his brainchild, and he felt that the original singers lacked a proper pop image. He hired the models Morvan and Pilatus to pose as Milli Vanilli's singers with the promise that they could sing on the next album.

The group's fans felt betrayed. Some launched class-action lawsuits to reclaim cash spent on albums and concerts. The Best New Artist Grammy was promptly withdrawn. Milli Vanilli's record label not only dropped the act—it deleted all of their songs. Morvan and Pilatus tried to redeem themselves by forming their own group, called Rob & Fab, and releasing an album on which they actually sang. It was a flop. Apparently, the former models were easier on the eyes than the ears.

OTHER *famous* PHONIES

LOKI

Our first fraudster is such a phony, he's not even real! Loki is a shape-changing god of lies and trickery in Norse mythology, fond of causing drama among the other deities. His troublemaking reaches its crescendo at Ragnarok, a world-ending battle royale of the gods. It's no wonder Marvel Comics created a more modern version of Loki as the sneaky nemesis (and stepbrother) of Thor.

QUIZ-SHOW CHEATERS

Just like today, game shows were popular TV entertainment back in the 1950s. But unlike today, many of them were rigged. The most famous case was a trivia show called *Twenty One*. Ratings slipped after a brainy-but-boring contestant named Herb Stempel went on a six-week winning streak, so the show's producer talked him into losing the game to Charles Van Doren, a more TV-friendly challenger. An audience favorite, Van Doren was given the questions and answers before each show so he would keep on winning. Eventually the truth came out, prompting the United States Congress to pass a law against phony game shows.

THE FOX SISTERS

Margaret, Kate, and Leah Fox became famous in the 19th century for acting as messengers—or "mediums" —between the dead and the living. They communicated with the dearly departed by rapping on table surfaces and getting knocking sounds in reply, a sort of Morse code from the morgue. These rap sessions brought the trio fame and followers. In 1888, however, Margaret Fox confessed that the whole thing was a sham. The girls were making the knocking noises by cracking their toes and knuckles. Despite her admission, belief in mediums continues today.

Hack Attack

The sneaky crimes of cyber swindlers

IT LETS YOU PLAY ADDICTING GAMES, KEEPS YOU IN THE LOOP WITH FRIENDS AND FAMILY, AND IS A BOTTOMLESS SOURCE OF CUTE-KITTY VIDEOS. Yes, the Internet is the greatest thing ever. But in the wrong hands, this global network of connected computers is a dangerous tool. So-called cyber criminals go online to steal, bully, spy, attack, and cause all sorts of trouble—all without leaving the house. Cyber crimes cost Americans as much as $100 billion each year! Here are five of the sneakiest examples of this fastest-growing kind of crime...

HACKING Tech-savvy troublemakers who try to gain unauthorized access to the computers of people, corporations, or governments are called hackers. Their most valuable possession isn't money or gadgets or even free video games. It's information! Hackers break into private networks to swipe secret info, which they can then sell or use for all sorts of dastardly purposes.
Famous case: A 16-year-old computer genius hacked into NASA in 2000 and swiped plans for the International Space Station.

CYBER WARFARE This is cyber crime on a grand scale: nations employing armies of hackers to swipe information, divert cash, shut down services, and wreak electronic havoc with enemy nations. It's a new type of warfare that can cripple an enemy country without firing a shot.
Famous case: In 2009, the United States Pentagon established the U.S. Cyber Command to defend the country from cyber attacks from foreign powers and initiate such attacks against foes.

CYBER-CRIME-FIGHTING TIPS

1) Don't open attachments in emails from people or companies you don't recognize.

2) Install antivirus software on your computer to keep it healthy, and keep your firewall on.

3) Studies show the most commonly used Internet passwords are just the user's name, the numbers 123456, or—believe it or not—the word "password." Never use any combination of these! The strongest passwords are at least eight characters long and include a combination of upper- and lower-case letters, numbers, and punctuation symbols. And treat your passwords like your gym socks—never share them with anybody!

SPREADING VIRUSES Viruses are nasty programs that slow down your computer, log everything you type, send your browser to undesirable websites, or shut off your system completely. In other words, they make your computer sick! The only way to "heal" it is with an antivirus program or, in the case of a fatal virus, wipe the hard drive clean and start over. Viruses infect your computer through emails or by hiding in programs you download.
Famous case: An email with the subject line "ILOVEYOU" broke a lot of hearts—and computers— in 2000 when it spread a nasty virus that erased files, changed browser home pages, and spread itself through the address book of computer users' email systems.

PHISHING This is an attempt by cyber crooks to trick people into revealing log-in information for online bank accounts and other secure sources of cash. Phishing often takes the form of sneaky emails created to look like they're from trusted friends or companies.
Famous case: An oldie-but-not-goodie scam involves an email from a phony "Nigerian prince" who promises a king's ransom if you send him bank-account info and enough money to help him transfer millions from his home country.

IDENTITY THEFT Identity thieves use every dirty cyber trick to impersonate you online. Once they've assumed your identity, the thieves can go on a shopping spree with your savings, sign you up for all sorts of unsavory services, and generally make a mess of your life.
Famous case: In 2012, a husband-and-wife team led a ring of identity thieves who swiped credit-card info from people around the world and handed it off to teams of shoppers who spent millions on luxury hotels, exotic cars, and even a private jet.

'STACHE'S SECRET

Hey, some of my best friends are hackers! So-called "white hat" hackers try to break into the networks of companies and government agencies just to probe them for weaknesses, which they report to the folks in charge. Some hackers get paid big bucks for this service!

play DOUGH

COUNTERFEITERS USE **SNEAKY TRICKS** TO CREATE **FUNNY MONEY**

THE LITTLE THINGS Real bills are covered with itty-bitty details—tight geometric shapes, tiny patches of text, red and blue fibers—that even high-definition printers cannot replicate accurately. Colors come out wrong, and fine features end up blotchy and blurry.

BILL PROTECTORS:
TRICKS THAT KEEP
U.S. CURRENCY REAL

PAPER TALE Currency is printed on a special type of paper made from cotton and linen, which is why your bills don't become blobs of papery mush when they're accidentally run through the wash. That unique paper (combined with the intense pressure of the printing presses) gives genuine money its thin, crisp, unique feel that's nearly impossible to replicate.

Bootlegged **BOOTY**

Counterfeiters copy more than just currency.
Here are the top five most commonly cloned goodies . . .

1) Designer handbags and wallets
2) Watches and jewelry
3) Name-brand clothing
4) Electronics and gadgets
5) Shoes

Unless you win the lottery, inherit a fortune, or love your job, making money is hard. Which is precisely why so many sneaks have tried *making* money through counterfeiting, or forging currency and trying to pass it off as the real thing.

No sooner was money invented than clever criminals began trying to copy it. In ancient Greece, counterfeiters would clip the edges off gold and silver coins and melt the shavings around worthless metal cores to create passable copies. Modern-day counterfeiters use high-tech copiers and high-resolution printers to create fake bills, which are often easy to detect for their funny paper quality. More technologically advanced crooks avoid the paper problem by bleaching the dollar symbols from small bills—$1s and $5s—and reprinting them with higher amounts.

Punishment for minting funny money has always been severe. From ancient times through the American Civil War, counterfeiters were often put to death. A country's entire economy depends on its citizens having faith in the value of its currency. Too much phony dough floating around in circulation could undermine that faith and cause the economy to crumble. Counterfeit cash is so dangerous that nations have even used it as a weapon in wartime—just another example of the power of money.

JUMPING JACKSON A second and much fainter portrait of President Andrew Jackson is barely visible to the right of his main image when you hold your bill to the light. This special type of hidden image is called a watermark.

STRIP SEARCH Visible on both sides of a $20 bill when you hold it to the light, this skinny thread is implanted vertically and imprinted with the tiny words "USA TWENTY." It also glows green under ultraviolet light.

TRICKY 20 Tilt your bill in the light and the small 20 in the bottom right corner of the front shifts from green to copper. It's printed with color-shifting ink.

VERY IMPORTANT DATE The U.S. Mint began redesigning currency with new security features—starting with the $100 bill—in 1996. Any cash still in circulation from before that year is much easier to copy.

'STACHE'S SECRET
The U.S. Secret Service is famous for protecting the president today, but it was originally begun in 1865 to investigate and stop counterfeiters.

AT LARGE!

FOLLOW THE TRAIL OF THREE FAMOUS FUGITIVES

HALT! FREEZE! HANDS UP! Such curt commands from authority figures mean only one thing to anyone desperate to dodge capture: Run! Some of history's sneakiest figures were "on the lam"—lead double fugitives forced to keep on the move, lead double (or triple or quadruple) lives, and become masters of disguise to stay ahead of the long arm of the law. We track down three of the sneakiest.

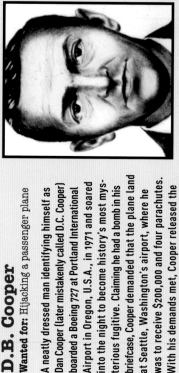

D.B. Cooper

Wanted for: Hijacking a passenger plane

A neatly dressed man identifying himself as Dan Cooper (later mistakenly called D.C. Cooper) boarded a Boeing 727 at Portland International Airport in Oregon, U.S.A., in 1971 and soared into the night to become history's most mysterious fugitive. Claiming he had a bomb in his briefcase, Cooper demanded that the plane land at Seattle, Washington's airport, where he was to receive $200,000 and four parachutes. With his demands met, Cooper released the passengers and ordered the pilots to take off and fly him to Mexico at the lowest speed and altitude possible. Once in the air, Cooper lowered the plane's rear stairs and parachuted into the rainy night over the wilderness of southwestern Washington.

Fate of the fugitive: Unknown! Although no body was found, FBI investigators believe that the hijacker who called himself Dan Cooper didn't survive his jump. A boy hiking near the jump site in 1980 stumbled upon $5,800 of the ransom cash, but the fate of the mysterious skyjacker and his money is still a mystery. Hoping to close the case once and for all, the FBI released new eyewitness sketches of Cooper in 2007. He's still wanted dead or alive.

MISSING!

Mary Read
Wanted for: Piracy in the Caribbean

In a golden age of sneaky pirates (the late 17th and early 18th centuries), Mary Read was one of the sneakiest. She took a liking to lying early, impersonating her late brother at a young age to weasel money from their grandmother. She maintained the dude ruse into adulthood, when she joined the military and fought fiercely alongside male soldiers who thought she was just one of the guys. Eventually she sailed to the Caribbean and turned pirate after siding with mutineers.

Still dressed in dude's duds, Read joined the crew of John "Calico Jack" Rackham, a charming, sharp-dressing real-life equivalent of Captain Jack Sparrow. She relished the pirate's life alongside Calico Jack and Anne Bonny, another famous female pirate. Read's "secret" was safe until Bonny, thinking Read was a dashing man, began to flirt with her—which made Calico Jack jealous. But the buccaneer captain was delighted when Read revealed she was really a woman. From that point on, he opened his ship's charter to female and male freebooters alike.

Fate of the fugitive: Captured!
When a pirate hunter pulled alongside Calico Jack's ship during a raucous pirate party, only Read and Bonny were brave enough to stand on deck and face their captors. Both women were sentenced to be hanged—the punishment for piracy—but they claimed they were pregnant to escape death. Read died in prison in 1721, near the end of the golden age of piracy.

Frank Abagnale
Wanted for: Committing fraud and impersonation

An airline pilot, teacher, doctor, and lawyer—all before the age of 21—Frank Abagnale had a resume that seemed too busy to be true. And it was! Abagnale was a master of making things up. After swindling banks by writing phony checks, he decided to impersonate an airline pilot so he could get free airfare—at age 16! He traveled the world for two years in the 1960s, charging hotel rooms and food to the airline, before deciding he needed a new identity to stay one step ahead of the law. Abagnale went on to impersonate a pediatrician and an attorney after forging a transcript from Harvard Law School. He even got a job at the Louisiana State Attorney General's office before his 20th birthday. An escape artist as well as a master of disguise, Abagnale gave police the slip twice before his luck finally ran out.

Fate of the fugitive: Reformed!
The master con artist was caught in France in 1969. He had to answer for fraud committed across the globe, serving sentences in French and Swedish prisons before getting sent back to the United States for more time behind bars. Today he's one of the good guys, helping banks and other businesses avoid imposters and crooks. His life story was turned into the 2002 Steven Spielberg movie *Catch Me If You Can.*

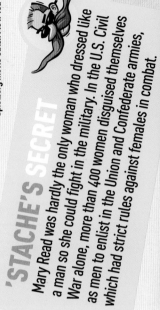

'STACHE'S SECRET
Mary Read was hardly the only woman who dressed like a man so she could fight in the military. In the U.S. Civil War alone, more than 400 women disguised themselves as men to enlist in the Union and Confederate armies, which had strict rules against females in combat.

MOST WANTED LIST

CAT BURGLARS

THE SNEAKIEST THIEVES

PETER SCOTT SCOFFED AT DOOR LOCKS. HE SAW DRAINPIPES AS LADDERS AND WINDOWS AS A WAY IN. He treated the newspaper's society pages like a catalog, noting where the well-to-do lived and the jewelry they wore. Scott was a cat burglar, one of

England's sneakiest. By the time he retired in the 1990s, he had stolen more than $30 million in jewels, furs, and artwork—including a priceless Picasso painting—from celebrities, aristocrats, and royalty. He was heralded as "King of the Cat Burglars" in the headlines. A 1965 movie chronicled his criminal exploits. In other words, he was hardly a common crook.

Cat burglars are a different breed of burglar, relying on their "catlike" stealth and climbing skills in pursuit of priceless possessions. (A famous Florida, U.S.A., burglar named Bill Mason

once skittered up a 15-story building in a storm—at night—to lift loot from a penthouse apartment.) Scott was known as the "human fly" for his ability to clamber up to the balconies and rooftops of London's more posh neighborhoods. And cat burglars are often cunning as well as sneaky. Scott dressed in an expensive suit before each break-in so he would fit in with the wealthy residents of the neighborhood. Once spotted by a rich homeowner while he was skulking downstairs, Scott peered up and said, "Everything's all right, madam." The woman wandered off thinking Scott was her butler.

He insisted he was a modern-day Robin Hood, robbing only from the rich. Truth was, Robin Hood gave to the poor; Scott did not. At the height of his thievery (and in between stints in prison for his crimes), Scott lived like the people he robbed. He spent every dime of his ill-gotten money on the good life: fancy cars, classy clothes, opulent homes. The King of the Cat Burglars died a pauper in 2013.

Sneaky Equipment:
BURGLARY GEAR

POLICE SCANNER
A radio that lets crooks eavesdrop on police chatter so they know when the cops are coming.

ASSORTED TOOLS
Burglars carry everything they might need—drills, hammers, screwdrivers, chisels—to dismantle doors, windows, and walls.

DIGITAL CAMERAS
Meticulous planners, cat burglars often snap high-resolution photos of places they case so they can study the photos for lapses in security.

LOCK PICKS
These slender strips of metal work like keys in the hands of a skilled burglar.

GLASS CUTTER
Tipped with a diamond bit, this tool slices circle-shaped holes in glass so thieves can undo window locks.

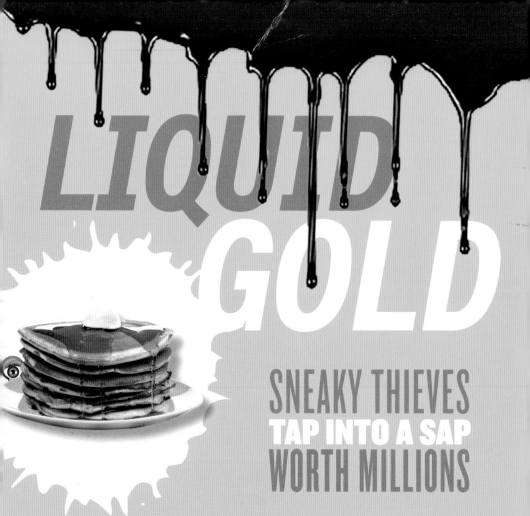

LIQUID GOLD

SNEAKY THIEVES
TAP INTO A SAP
WORTH MILLIONS

THE THIEVES STRUCK IN BROAD DAYLIGHT, PARKING THEIR TRUCKS AT THE LOADING DOCK OF A WAREHOUSE SOUTHWEST OF QUEBEC CITY, CANADA. They didn't need to dodge guards or disable alarms; the warehouse had little in the way of security. Inside was a golden treasure. The thieves took their time loading the loot, and they didn't spill a drop. It was a heist of Hollywood proportions (in fact, it inspired a movie). The thieves had stolen 16,000 barrels of maple syrup. And while a sweet-and-sticky pancake topping isn't typical treasure,

it's still a rare and valuable commodity. Maple sap can only be tapped from trees during a brief period each spring. It's not suitably sweet until it undergoes a time-consuming boiling process. One bad year can cause a shortage of syrup and a spike in its prices. Quebec is the world's leading producer of the sweet sap, and the Federation of Quebec Maple Syrup Producers maintains a reserve to make sure it never stops flowing to the stores. Who knew the maple-syrup business was so complicated? The thieves certainly did. And they knew

THREE-COURSE STEAL

MORE TASTY HEISTS

THE ENTRÉE
Two employees at a food distributor decided to take their work home with them when they loaded a rental truck with $65,000 worth of frozen chicken wings.

THE SIDE DISH
Thieves cut through the side of a delivery truck in England and stole 6,400 tins of baked beans while the truck's driver snoozed in the front seat.

AND FOR DESSERT . . .
A thief in Austria posing as a truck driver stole 18 tons of chocolate from a factory. Workers at the factory knew they'd been robbed when the real driver showed up.

that the Federation kept a syrup reserve in a warehouse in the small town of Saint-Louis-de-Blandford. Instead of plotting an elaborate break-in, they simply rented a nearby section of the warehouse for a bogus business. That allowed them to park their trucks at the warehouse without arousing suspicion. The thieves could take their time siphoning off the liquid gold. Federation officials didn't even know they were being robbed until a semiannual inspection of the warehouse revealed that the syrup in the barrels had been replaced with water. The thieves, meanwhile, were posing as distributors, selling their stolen foodstuff to other provinces and across the border into the United States. But Canadians take the syrup business seriously (this wasn't the first syrup heist, although it was the largest). Authorities—including the Royal Canadian Mounted Police—questioned hundreds of people. Within two years, the gang of syrup stealers found themselves in a sticky mess: They'd all been arrested.

THAT's *NOT Sneaky*

SHOPPER SPENDS A PHONY FORTUNE

One totally uncool customer tried to buy $1,600 worth of Walmart merchandise in 2004 using a phony $1 million bill—and then had the gall to ask for change. Seems like the perfect crime, right? Not quite. The U.S. Treasury doesn't even make a denomination that big. (The bogus bill was actually a novelty-store gag gift.) The woman insisted she thought it was real—a gift from her husband—but she was still arrested for trying to pass off the funny money.

LYIN' ZOO LION

A Chinese zoo had some explaining to do when the furry beast behind the bars of its "African lion" exhibit barked instead of roared. Turns out the lion was actually a Tibetan mastiff dog, and it wasn't the only counterfeit creature on display (a white fox stalked the leopard cage and rats sat in a case meant for snakes). Keepers apologized for the ruse and promised to reopen the zoo with a legit lion.

PHONY DEATH HAS A FATAL FLAW

A Texas, U.S.A., woman helped fake the death of her husband to collect money from his insurance policy (and also to keep him out of jail for a previous charge), but she messed up one important detail. After the couple dug up a dead body and placed it in a wrecked car, the woman reported her husband dead in the crash. The police thought the story was fishy, so they tested the body—and discovered it was female.

Sometimes the police need to act just as sneaky as the crooks they catch. In the London borough of Brent, cops booby-trapped a car with a device that sprays SmartWater, an invisible, odorless chemical that glows green under ultraviolet light. A crook that broke into the car thought he'd gotten away with his crime until he was nabbed by police and exposed to the special light. He'd been caught green-handed!

CRIME FIGHTING GOES GREEN

CROOK CAUGHT DEAD AND ALIVE

When he heard the police pull up outside, a burglar who broke into a funeral home in Spain thought he could hide in plain sight by crawling into a display case and playing dead. He had just two problems: He was wearing normal street clothes instead of the formal duds normally adorning the deceased, and he was still breathing. The observant cops hauled the possum-playing burglar off to jail.

HOME INVADER MAKES A BAD CALL

A Maryland, U.S.A., thief left behind more than just fingerprints when he fled the scene of a crime. Police found his cell phone charging in a house he had just burglarized. Detectives called one of the phone's contacts to discover the name of the forgetful burglar, whom they tracked down and arrested.

CRUMMY CRIMINALS AND SORRY SCAMS THAT DIDN'T FOOL ANYBODY . . .

BURGLAR REPORTS HIS OWN CRIME

It wasn't the homeowner who called 911 when he found a stranger in his home in Portland, Oregon, U.S.A.—it was the burglar! Fearing that the owner had a weapon, the intruder locked himself in the bathroom and called the police, who promptly arrived and arrested the bungling burglar.

KNIT WIT: Even a five-year-old can sport a five o'clock shadow with a "Beard Head," a beanie with a built-in beard. The knitted facial hair comes in many varieties—from chin-hugging stubble to chest-length "barbarian" beards made of yarn. This product gets a seal of approval from Secret Agent 'Stache.

BUSTED BANDIT: A British crook thought he'd found the perfect disguise when he put a bag over his head to rob a gas station. There was only one problem: The bag was made of clear plastic! He was arrested two days later when a police officer recognized the crook from security-camera footage.

AIR FARCE: Flight attendants noticed something fishy about an elderly man who boarded their Air Canada plane in Hong Kong in 2011: His hands looked remarkably young. Their suspicions were confirmed when the passenger emerged from the plane's bathroom as a man in his 20s. Hoping to sneak into Canada under an assumed identity, the sneaky passenger had boarded the plane wearing an old-man mask.

DIRTY ROTTEN
Scoundrels

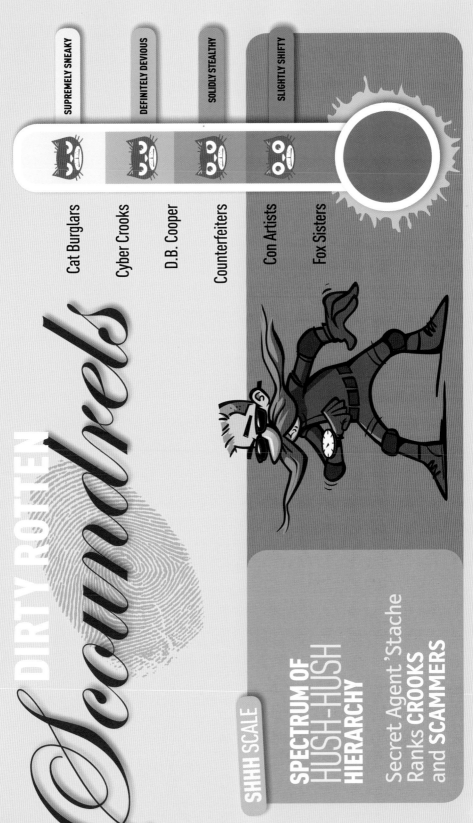

SUPREMELY SNEAKY

DEFINITELY DEVIOUS

SOLIDLY STEALTHY

SLIGHTLY SHIFTY

Cat Burglars

Cyber Crooks

D.B. Cooper

Counterfeiters

Con Artists

Fox Sisters

SHHH SCALE

SPECTRUM OF HUSH-HUSH HIERARCHY

Secret Agent 'Stache Ranks **CROOKS** and **SCAMMERS**

CHAPTER 4

Sneak Attack!

YOU'D EXPECT A BOOK CALLED *THE ART OF WAR* TO BE A BEST SELLER AMONG GENERALS AND MILITARY BUFFS, but this 2,500-year-old tome—written by a Chinese tactician named Sun Tzu—is also a big hit with executives, lawyers, coaches, and anyone else who works in a competitive career. Despite its scary title, the book isn't about waging big battles. Instead, it teaches how to *avoid* battles by outwitting the enemy using sneakiness and smarts. Sun Tzu would probably approve of the sly strategies and stealthy technologies revealed in this chapter.

DRASTIC

FIVE VICTORIES THROUGH DECEIT

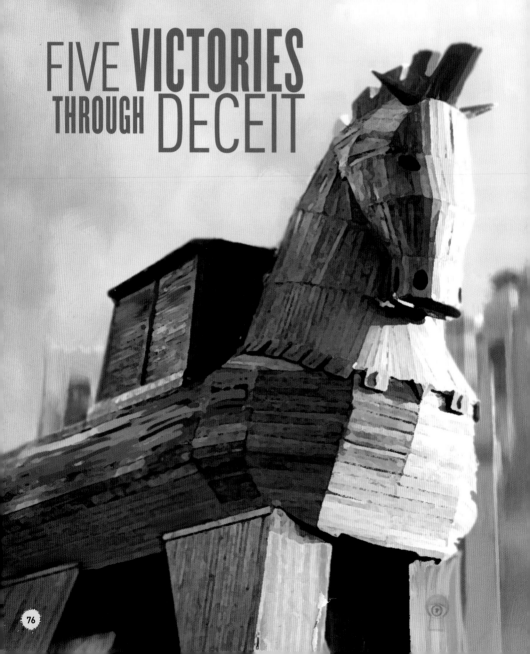

TACTICS

HORSING AROUND

LOCATION: **THE ANCIENT CITY OF TROY**

DATE: **CIRCA 1200 B.C.**

DETAILS OF THE DECEPTION: After laying siege to the city of Troy for a decade with nothing to show for it, the armies of Greece packed up their camp, boarded their ships, and headed for home. But they left a parting gift: a titanic wooden horse parked right outside Troy's gates.

You probably know what happened next. The Trojan Horse is the most famous case of a "ruse of war," or the use of deceit to achieve victory. Relieved that the long siege was over, the citizens of Troy hauled the horse into their city and partied late into the night. As the Trojans slept off their celebration, Greek soldiers hidden in the horse's belly emerged and opened the city gates. The Greek army, which had only pretended to sail home, swarmed into Troy and conquered it.

Whether the horse really existed or is just a tale from Greek mythology, its legend has inspired our language, our art, and even our software. A Trojan horse is the name for any computer program that's supposed to do one thing but secretly attacks your computer. Unlike the Trojans, at least, you have antivirus programs to protect you.

LESSON LEARNED: "Beware of Greeks bearing gifts," or so goes a translation of dialogue from the ancient poem *Aeneid*, which contains the tale of the Trojan Horse.

FACE-OFF IN THE MIDDLE EAST

LOCATION: **THE ANCIENT CITY OF BABYLON**

DATE: **CIRCA 500 B.C.**

DETAILS OF THE DECEPTION: When the high-ranking Persian soldier Zopyrus said he would do anything to help his commander, Darius the Great, conquer the great city of Babylon, he meant it! After cutting up his face, the bloodied Zopyrus appeared at the gates of Babylon claiming he'd been mutilated by Darius and wanted to defect to the other side. The horrified Babylonians opened their gates and even let Zopyrus join their army. The defaced "double agent" worked from the inside to weaken Babylon's defenses in secret. Darius the Great returned to conquer the city, and Zopyrus was well rewarded for his cunning—but painful—plan.

LESSON LEARNED: Double agents will do anything to build trust.

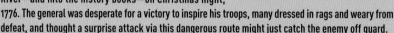

FIGHTING FOUNDING FATHER

LOCATION: **TRENTON, NEW JERSEY, U.S.A.**
DATE: **A.D. 1776**

DETAILS OF THE DECEPTION: Dodging floating chunks of ice in the dark and paddling through bone-chilling sleet, General George Washington led his force of roughly 2,400 Continental Army soldiers across the freezing Delaware River—and into the history books—on Christmas night, 1776. The general was desperate for a victory to inspire his troops, many dressed in rags and weary from defeat, and thought a surprise attack via this dangerous route might just catch the enemy off guard.

The tactic worked. Washington's men managed to surprise and defeat an encampment of British-paid German mercenaries in Trenton, New Jersey. Victory at the "Battle of Trenton" boosted morale and recruitment for the Continental Army. It's one of history's most famous sneak attacks.

LESSON LEARNED: Never underestimate an army when it's down (especially when it's led by George Washington).

GREIF STRICKEN

LOCATION: **BELGIUM**
DATE: **A.D. 1944**

DETAILS OF THE DECEPTION: When Germany's Adolf Hitler wanted to take control of crucial bridges in Belgium, he hatched one of World War II's sneakiest schemes: Operation Greif. Led by Otto Skorzeny, Hitler's most cunning commando, the mission involved dressing German troops in the uniforms of American soldiers (their foes) and sneaking them behind enemy lines, along with captured U.S. tanks and vehicles.

Skorzeny was unable to gather enough vehicles and English-speaking troops to succeed in destroying the bridges, but his disguised men still managed to confuse U.S. forces. They messed with road signs, passed along phony orders, and spread paranoia among their foes. U.S. soldiers began to question whether any allies they met were secretly Germans in disguise, which resulted in fatal cases of mistaken identity and at least one high-ranking U.S. officer being grilled at gunpoint until he could prove who he was.

LESSON LEARNED: Telling friend from foe in war is always tough (which is why many soldiers in WWII were given code words).

'STACHE'S SECRET

German commando Otto Skorzeny was charged with war crimes after WWII for dressing his troops in U.S. uniforms—a possible violation of established rules of war (yes, war has rules). But the charges were dropped after Skorzeny proved that his men changed back into German uniforms before fighting.

STINKY SECRET ENTRANCE

LOCATION: **THE FRENCH CASTLE CHATEAU GAILLARD**

DATE: **SUMMER OF A.D. 1203**

DETAILS OF THE DECEPTION: French attackers used every siege tactic in the book when they set upon the English-held Chateau Gaillard. Starving the castle's inhabitants and digging a mine to collapse a tower in the outer wall wasn't enough. The French forces still needed to find a way through the inner wall. One crafty soldier saw an easy way in: a toilet drain high up the wall. He and a small band of men climbed up the drain, crawled through the toilet seat cut into the stone, then opened the gates for the attackers. Siege engines battered the last of the castle's defenses, and Chateau Gaillard finally fell to the French.

LESSON LEARNED: If your castle comes under siege, plug those drains!

Silent BUT VIOLENT

Ninja **MYTH** vs. Ninja **FACT**

MYTH	FACT
Ninja could walk on water.	Ninja wore bucketlike shoes on their feet to cross castle moats.
Ninja could vanish in the blink of an eye.	Early masters of gunpowder, ninja wielded smoke bombs to hide their escape.
Ninja could fly.	They couldn't soar through the air, but ninja supposedly mastered a secret speedy walk that required no more energy than a regular pace.

'STACHE'S SECRET

Japanese legend tells of a ninja who hid in the cesspit beneath a warlord's outhouse, then attacked from below when the warlord took a bathroom break. Talk about a dirty trick!

When Ninja Ruled the Night

Protected by his loyal samurai warriors and surrounded by sheer castle walls, the Japanese warlord thought he was safe from his enemies.

He was wrong.

Outside his castle, a mercenary clad in black slides from shadow to shadow in the twilight. He carries with him all the tools he needs for tonight's dirty duty. He is a ninja—also known as a shinobi—trained since childhood in the arts of stealth, espionage, and assassination. Like all men and women who entered the ninja trade, he was feared and despised for his sneaky tactics and supposed supernatural powers. According to legend, ninja could fly, walk on water, and vanish. Only one of these feats was false.

The roots of the ninja stretch back to the 8th century—to secretive mountain clans trained in survival, self-defense, stealth, and evasion. (In one early legend, a 13-year-old ninja escaped his pursuers by climbing a bamboo tree until it swayed to the opposite bank of a river.) These secretive warriors emerged from the shadows in the 16th century, when hundreds of power-hungry warlords squabbled over control of Japan. During this violent "feudal" era, warlords relied on their armies of samurai—noble warriors whose code of battle forbade sneaky tactics—to defend their lands and attack rivals. But when they needed to spy on, assassinate, and create confusion among rivals, the warlords hired ninja.

Two villages in central Japan—Iga and Koga—were centers of ninja training. The shinobi business boomed in the 16th century, as ninja hired themselves out to the highest bidder. A ninja might work for a warlord one year, then spy on that same warlord the next. A ninja on a mission needed to blend in anywhere, from a bustling village to a castle rooftop at midnight. That meant he or she was a master of disguise. Ninja would dress as farmers, merchants, or musicians to slip unnoticed through the countryside. In one famous siege, a team of ninja dressed as the castle's guards and marched right through the front gate, set fire to the fortress, then escaped as the inhabitants bickered over who started the flames.

The ninja on tonight's mission is infiltrating the castle solo. Using a bamboo tube as a snorkel, he crosses the castle's moat like a ghost, then unrolls his tobibashigo—a throwable rope ladder with hooks on the end—to scale the sheer wall. It's midnight, and this ninja's work has just begun.

NINJA GEAR

DEADLY DUDS

COWL Two pieces of dark fabric covered the ninja's hooded face except for the eyes. Many ninja also carried straw hats to help hide their identity by day and keep their heads dry in the rain.

SUIT A ninja's jacket and pants—an ensemble of dark fabric called a shinobi shozoku—were kept tidy by a long cloth belt, with no dangling clasps to snag on obstacles while climbing, fighting, or fleeing. Some ninja wore chain-link armor under their outfit to blunt blows from blade-wielding foes.

A NINJA ON A MISSION WAS LIKE AN ARMY OF ONE, able to live off the land and adapt to any danger far from home base. That meant these wary warriors had to haul everything they might need to spy, infiltrate, and attack.

SHOES Ninja boots—called tabi—were stuffed with cotton for stealthy stepping and had a split toe that made climbing easier.

'STACHE'S SECRET

The fabric of a ninja's suit was actually dark navy instead of true black, the better to blend in with the moonlight.

TEKAGI Ninja attached these hooks to ropes and used them like grappling hooks to climb walls or shimmy across moats.

WICKED WEAPONRY

SHURIKEN These blade-tipped metal discs—aka "throwing stars"—have become the ninja's calling card in karate movies, in which black-clad assassins whiz shuriken at foes with terrifying accuracy. In reality, they were used only to slow pursuers. Wouldn't you think twice about chasing a ninja if she started chucking razor-tipped stars in your direction?

KATANA Ninja weaponry was often modeled after the arsenal of the noble samurai, except adapted for a darker purpose. Case in point: The ninja sword, called a katana, was similar to a samurai's blade but shorter. That made it easier to swing in cramped quarters and left room in the scabbard to stash blinding powder that could be flung at an enemy's eyes.

TETSUBISHI Another weapon for discouraging hot pursuit, this tiny metal lump had sharpened points that faced up when tossed on the ground (like a toy jack adapted for danger). Ninja dropped them while fleeing the scene, giving anyone who gave chase a case of sore feet.

KURASI-GAMA Modified from a farming tool, this short bamboo pole had a sickle on one end and a long weighted chain on the other. As was typical with ninja gear, the kurasi-gama had multiple uses. It worked as a weapon (the chain swept enemies off their feet) or as a tool for climbing.

UTILITY BAG Ninjas on the go carried healing potions and poisons, food pills, and stone pens for copying castle maps and writing in secret codes. They also packed a special folded-up towel that did triple duty as a bandage, a sling for injured limbs, and...well, a towel for drying off.

STEALTHY TOOLS

SAOTO HIKIGANE Today's spies rely on high-tech microphones to eavesdrop on the enemy, but ninja warriors used a much simpler tool. This metal cylinder let them listen through walls to discover the location of guards and overhear secret conversations.

TEKKO-KAGI When it came time to climb, ninja slipped iron spikes onto the palms of their hands and the soles of their boots. The spikes gripped the mortar and wood in castle walls, granting a ninja the climbing ability rivaling Spider-Man's. The claws also worked as a weapon and could deflect sword attacks.

SNEAK SPEAK

How "code talkers" wielded words to win a war

ONE OF THE MIGHTIEST SECRET WEAPONS OF WORLD WAR II WASN'T A STEALTHY PLANE or an experimental gun or some strength-granting super-soldier serum. It was language.

Communication is crucial in any battle. Commanders must issue orders to soldiers, sailors, and pilots, who in turn need to provide a big picture of the battle at hand. Lack of communication creates the dreaded "fog of war," a perilous situation in which confusion reigns on the battlefield and troops can't tell allies from enemies. But communication is worthless—even dangerous—if it gets intercepted by the other side. It's hard to plan a sneak attack when your foes tune in to every radio transmission.

To throw off eavesdroppers, countries embroiled in World War II developed

But the U.S. military found a foolproof secret language not from a machine, but from America's original residents.

Native Americans speak complex languages that are virtually unknown outside their tribes. Since the First World War, they've used their unique linguistic abilities in the U.S. military's signal corps as "code talkers," translating sensitive communications into their language and transmitting them much faster than any machine. Even if enemies learned to decode Cherokee, Comanche, Navajo, Choctaw, or any of the other code-talker languages, they would still need to figure out the secret terms for words that didn't exist in those languages. The Navajo word for "iron fish," for instance, was used to describe submarines. A tank became "turtle" in Comanche. Their term for Adolf Hitler: "Crazy White Man."

The code talkers' mission was so

84

MYSTERY MACHINES
FAMOUS ENCRYPTION CONTRAPTIONS

"encryption machines" (see sidebar) that converted crucial messages into secret codes, which were then deciphered by recipients with the same machine. There's just one problem: Encryption systems—even the most complex ones—could be cracked given enough time and resources.

top secret they weren't even allowed to share details with their loved ones. Their existence was finally declassified in 1968 (23 years after the close of the war), but it would take several decades before they were recognized for their crucial role in winning World War II.

ENIGMA MACHINE
Wheels inside this device scrambled messages typed via keyboard into a code that the Germans in World War II considered impossible to crack. Polish "cryptologists" reverse engineered their own machine and cracked the code before the war even started.

PURPLE
Despite warnings from their German allies, the Japanese in World War II refused to believe the United States had deciphered the cipher for their "Purple" encryption machine. The U.S. military's name for their code-cracking project: Magic.

U.S. ARMY M-209
This lunch-box-size encryption system was light and portable—perfect for sending coded messages from the battlefield. The Germans had deciphered its coding system, but the U.S. military knew more on its code talkers and their indecipherable language.

SECRET SOLDIERS:
THE SPECIAL FORCES

THE NINJA MAY HAVE VANISHED LONG AGO (EXCEPT FOR A FEW NINJA-CLAN DESCENDANTS WHO CARRY ON SHINOBI TRADITIONS IN JAPAN), BUT THEIR SNEAKY SPIRIT LIVES ON IN A NEW BREED OF WARRIOR: THE SPECIAL FORCES.

Many countries handpick troops and train them in survival, stealth, and the use of specialized gear. These elite soldiers are too valuable to waste on run-of-the-mill military missions. Instead, they're dispatched on special operations, also known as spec-ops.

The use of elite troops goes back centuries. The Roman navy crewed sleek camouflaged boats with handpicked sailors for scouting missions. During the Middle Ages, British lords employed "sappers" to dig secret tunnels beneath enemy castles to bring down the walls. But special forces as we know them evolved during World War II. Each country in that conflict formed elite groups of troops for specialized missions (Canada's Devil's Brigade, for instance, infiltrated enemy alpine wilderness on skis) and for lengthy missions far from home base. Today, spec-ops troops are sent to rescue hostages, sabotage enemy installations, and gather information on the enemy—often in the dead of night.

SELECTIVE SERVICE

The special forces don't accept just any regular G.I. Joe or Jane. The U.S. Navy SEALs, for instance, recommends that its applicants achieve the following physical-fitness feats before applying . . .

ACTIVITY	RECOMMENDED RESULT
Swim 500 yards (457 m) breast- or sidestroke	Under 9:30 minutes
Completed push-ups in two minutes	100
Completed sit-ups in two minutes	100
Total completed pull-ups with no time limit	25
Run 1.5 miles (2.4 km) in boots and long pants	Under 9:30 minutes

And that's just the admittance test for SEAL training. Once accepted, candidates endure a grueling seven-month program that teaches sneaky combat skills for use on sea, in the air, and on land (thus the letters in the SEAL name) while being pushed to their physical and mental limits. Only about 20 percent of the candidates make it through training to become a SEAL.

WHO'S SNEAKIER: SEALS OR NINJA?

When a six-year-old Virginia first grader debated with a chum over who was stealthier, Navy SEALs or ninja, he went to a higher authority. He mailed the question to Admiral William McRaven, a former SEAL and head of U.S. Special Operations Command. To everyone's surprise, McRaven answered: "I think ninjas are probably quieter than SEALs, but we are better swimmers and also better with guns and blowing things up."

SPEC-OPS GEAR

SPECIAL-FORCES TROOPS ARE THE BEST OF THE BEST IN THEIR NATION'S MILITARY, so it makes sense that they're issued the best of the best in equipment for their sneaky missions. Such as …

NIGHT-VISION/INFRARED GOGGLES

These high-tech goggles amplify all the night's lights—car headlamps, streetlights, the moon, and even starlight—to illuminate the night landscape in an eerie green glow. Some models also detect infrared light to highlight the heat of human bodies far away or even behind concrete walls.

SUPPRESSOR

Guns go *bang, bang, bang,* which makes it awfully hard to sneak around. Suppressors quiet the thunder of gunfire to a dull *thunk, thunk, thunk.*

COMMUNICATIONS GEAR

Modern spec-ops forces carry global-positioning devices to keep tabs on their locations as well as satellite radios to communicate with each other and home base from any location. Special "bone phones" transmit sound through the bones in their head and don't "leak" noise like standard headphones.

BODY ARMOR

Before they enter dangerous territory, special forces members slip on special vests with pockets for plates made of bulletproof material. The plates weigh roughly six pounds (2.7 kg) each, which adds up fast, so operators carry only as much as they think they'll need for adequate protection.

SEAL DELIVERY VEHICLE

The U.S. Navy SEALs excel at being sneaky underwater, using specialized "rebreather" scuba gear that doesn't leave a trail of bubbles. But air tanks run empty, and even the fittest SEALs tire after a long swim, so the Navy developed a tiny submarine to transport SEALs undetected into the mission area. Not much larger than a torpedo and open to the water (the SEALs still need to wear masks and breathe from regulators), the Seal Delivery Vehicle is launched from the back of a larger submarine.

COMBAT CANINE

Your pooch might know how to sit and roll over, but can she parachute into enemy territory? Highly trained "military working dogs" often accompany special forces on their missions. Typically of the stocky Belgian shepherd Malinois breed, these tough mutts wear bulletproof armor equipped with cameras so they can scout ahead or send pictures from hard-to-reach places. They even wear protective goggles—called "doggles."

Worn aboard ships at sea
by the U.S. Navy

Worn in forests and jungles
by the Honduran Army

Worn in desert environments
by the Italian Army

Worn in snowy environments
by the Finnish Defense Force

Sea Sight: "Dazzled" SHIPS

Deceive THE Eye

BELIEVE IT OR NOT, THE BIG SHIP YOU SEE CRUISING IN THE ABOVE PHOTO IS SUPPOSED TO BE CAMOUFLAGED—BUT WITH A DESIGN MEANT TO DRAW ATTENTION TO THE VESSEL RATHER THAN MAKE IT VANISH.

The ship was painted with a striking scheme known as razzle-dazzle: a riot of intersecting stripes, odd shapes, and vibrant colors reminiscent of a splitting migraine. The United States and British navies adopted these blinding designs to disguise their warships during World War I (from 1914 to 1918).

Today's naval gunners use radar, laser range finders, and computers to lock on to enemy ships with terrifying accuracy, but during World War I such targeting tasks were done largely with the naked eye. Gunners needed to spot enemy vessels and determine their course and speed, then fire shells and torpedoes in the direction they hoped the enemy was headed. But ships carrying the razzle-dazzle treatment were difficult to identify and plot. The crisscrossing stripes and striking shapes tricked the eye, making it tough to tell back (stern) from front (bow).

No two paint jobs were the same, and many were designed by artists (whose designs later inspired famous pieces of art). Military historians aren't certain of the effectiveness of razzle-dazzle camouflage, but it certainly made for the most strikingly colored fleets in the history of warfare.

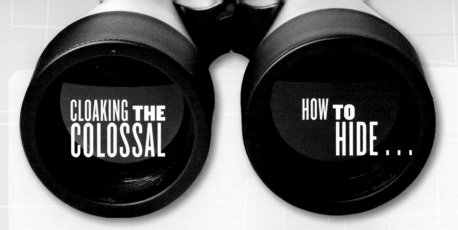

CLOAKING **THE** COLOSSAL

HOW **TO** HIDE . . .

. . . A TANK

Rumbling along like gas-powered earthquakes, tanks are much too heavy, loud, and smelly (from their exhaust) to sneak past the five senses, but an experimental type of "active" camouflage called Adaptiv helps them hide in plain sight. Small hexagonal plates covering the tank heat or cool instantly to match the background temperature, disguising the tank as a harmless object on the heat sensors of enemy targeting systems.

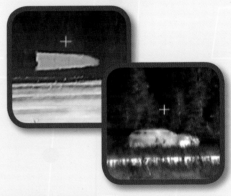

. . . A SUBMARINE

Sneaking under the sea in a submersible vessel isn't as easy as you'd think. Submarines might be out of sight from the surface, but sound travels faster and farther underwater. Propellers, power tools, and even crew chatter and dropped silverware create a racket that gives away a sub's position on arrays of underwater microphones used to monitor for them. Modern subs are built to run silent and deep, with ultraquiet engines and noise-baffling hulls. Such so-called "stealth subs" end their missions not with a bang, but with a whisper.

. . . A PLANE

Early forms of fighter-plane and bomber camouflage included paint schemes to match the ground from above and arrays of lights to blend with the daylight sky from below. But these systems are simple tricks compared to the sneaky, state-of-the-art technology you'll read about when you turn the page.

UNDER THE RADAR

THE EVOLUTION OF STEALTHY CRAFT

LEAST STEALTHY

U-2 SPY PLANE

First flown: **1955**
Used by: **U.S. Air Force, the Central Intelligence Agency, NASA, Taiwanese military**

One of the first planes designed to spy on other countries undetected, the U-2 soars so high that pilots must wear pressurized space suits. The U-2's designers thought radar couldn't track planes above 70,000 feet (21,000 m). They were wrong. Several were shot down.

The U-2 program was strictly hush-hush, so imagine the surprise of an Air Force commander when one of these odd birds made an emergency landing at his New Mexico, U.S.A., base in 1956 and out climbed a pilot wearing a space suit.

SR-71 BLACKBIRD

First flown: **1964**
Used by: **U.S. Air Force, NASA**

Test-flown at the mysterious "Area 51" government facility in the Nevada desert, the Blackbird is designed to fly higher (up to 90,000 feet) and faster (three times the speed of sound) than any other plane. It carries high-tech cameras for capturing detailed, close-up photos of military bases and other strategic sites worth snapping.

The Blackbird is coated with a special black paint (hence its name) that soaks up radar beams.

RAH-66 COMANCHE

First flown: **1996**
Used by: **U.S. Army as a prototype**

Helicopters are inherently not stealthy because of their large and loud rotors (propellers are like mirrors for radar beams). This prototype stealth chopper has a skin of special materials that absorbs radar signals, while weapons are hidden inside hatches to create a smaller radar target.

A conventional helicopter's thunderous rotor goes *whup-whup-whup*. The Comanche's special five-blade rotor, however, whispers *wush-wush-wush*. Targets on the ground never hear it coming.

WHEN IT COMES TO THE ARTS OF ESPIONAGE AND WAR, IT'S BEST TO REMAIN UNSEEN AND UNHEARD. Any nation able to deploy troops and attack craft undetected beyond the borders of other countries gains a huge tactical advantage. In that sense, sneakiness is the ultimate weapon.

There's just one big obstacle: radar. This decades-old technology uses invisible beams of light to detect intruders on the ocean, in the sky, and even in space. Radar beams bounce off objects—planes, cars, boats, missiles, flocks of birds, runaway balloons—and paint a simple picture of these "intruders" on the operator's screen back at the radar-broadcasting station. With such systems in place, every country can keep an eye on its coasts and airspace for uninvited guests.

Unless those guests use stealth technology. Since the 1940s, engineers have been working in secret labs across the globe to develop materials and designs that make certain vehicles— especially planes, helicopters, and ships—invisible to radar. Here's a sampling of these crafty craft...

MOST **STEALTHY**

VISBY-CLASS CORVETTE

First sailed: **2009**
Used by: **Swedish Navy**

Radar beams work best when they have broad surfaces to bounce off of, which is why many modern "stealth" vehicles have angular designs that scatter radar energy in every direction except back at the station. The Visby-class combat vessel is a perfect example. Its angular shape—like something out of a 3-D video game—has a low "radar signature."

The Visby-class vessel's gun turret retracts when not in use to reduce the boat's visibility on radar.

F-35 LIGHTNING II

First flown: **2006**
Used by: **U.S. military, Royal Air Force**

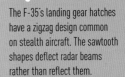

Decades of stealth-technology research have gone into this sleek jet, built for reconnaissance, dog-fighting other planes, and midnight raids behind enemy lines. The F-35's angular, low-profile shape deflects radar beams, while its airframe is constructed of top secret materials that absorb radar energy. The jet is even hard to spot with heat-seeking sensors and the naked eye, making it the sky's ultimate master of disguise.

The F-35's landing gear hatches have a zigzag design common on stealth aircraft. The sawtooth shapes deflect radar beams rather than reflect them.

SNEAK DETECTORS: Japanese warlords "ninja-proofed" their castles with special floors that squeaked under sneaky feet. Nails arranged along the underside of each creaky floorboard rubbed against metal clamps to produce a chirping sound (which is why the floors were called "nightingale floors").

CURVY CORRIDORS: The halls leading to important chambers in many Japanese castles twisted and turned to slow down and confuse intruders. These mazelike corridors cost ninja precious time in which they were more likely to be captured.

SPRING BREAK: When all else failed and the fear of ninja attack became unbearable, many warlords simply packed up their households and fled to secret hot springs far from their castles. A soothing soak cured their ninjaphobia, but many warlords had a tricky time ruling their lands while on vacation.

CUNNING Combat

SPECTRUM OF HUSH-HUSH HIERARCHY

Secret Agent 'Stache Ranks **SNEAKY ATTACKS**

SUPREMELY SNEAKY	DEFINITELY DEVIOUS	SOLIDLY STEALTHY	SLIGHTLY SHIFTY
Ninja	F-35 Lightning II Stealth Fighter	Special Forces	Code Talkers	Dazzled Ships

95

CHAPTER 5

Spy Craft

SPIES IN MOVIES ARE SUAVE AND SUPERHUMAN, SHARP DRESSERS AND SMOOTH TALKERS. But real-life secret agents steer clear of spiffy duds and iffy situations, silly one-liners and kung-fu confrontations. When you work in the world of espionage—the business of stealing secrets—standing out from the crowd could get you locked up. See for yourself as we infiltrate the shadowy realm of spies, revealing their top-secret tactics, declassifying their cool tools—even blowing the cover of a real-life secret agent!

SPY EXAM

THE INS AND OUTS OF **INTERNATIONAL ESPIONAGE**

CALL THEM SPOOKS, SECRET AGENTS, CASE OFFICERS, OPERATIVES, INTELLIGENCE ASSETS—THEY'RE ALL SPIES, OR PROFESSIONAL SNOOPS WHO TRY TO SNIFF OUT SECRET INFORMATION FROM GOVERNMENTS, MILITARY ORGANIZATIONS, AND COMPANIES (A SPECIAL SORT OF SPYING CALLED CORPORATE ESPIONAGE). It's not a new job. Ancient Egypt hired spies to keep an eye on its enemies. So did the Greeks and Romans. It's hardly part-time work, either. Spies keep busy in times of war and peace. Some do it for the money, love of their country, or hatred of a rival nation, but they all have one thing in common: A spy's life is full of lies. Here's a top secret primer on these expert sneaks.

SPY AGENCIES ACROSS THE GLOBE

United States: Central Intelligence Agency (CIA)
Mexico: Centro de Investigación y Seguridad Nacional (CISEN)
China: Ministry of State Security (MSS)
Former Soviet Union: Komitet Gosudarstvennoy Bezopasnosti (KGB)
Israel: Mossad
Kenya: National Intelligence Service
United Kingdom: Secret Intelligence Service (MI6)

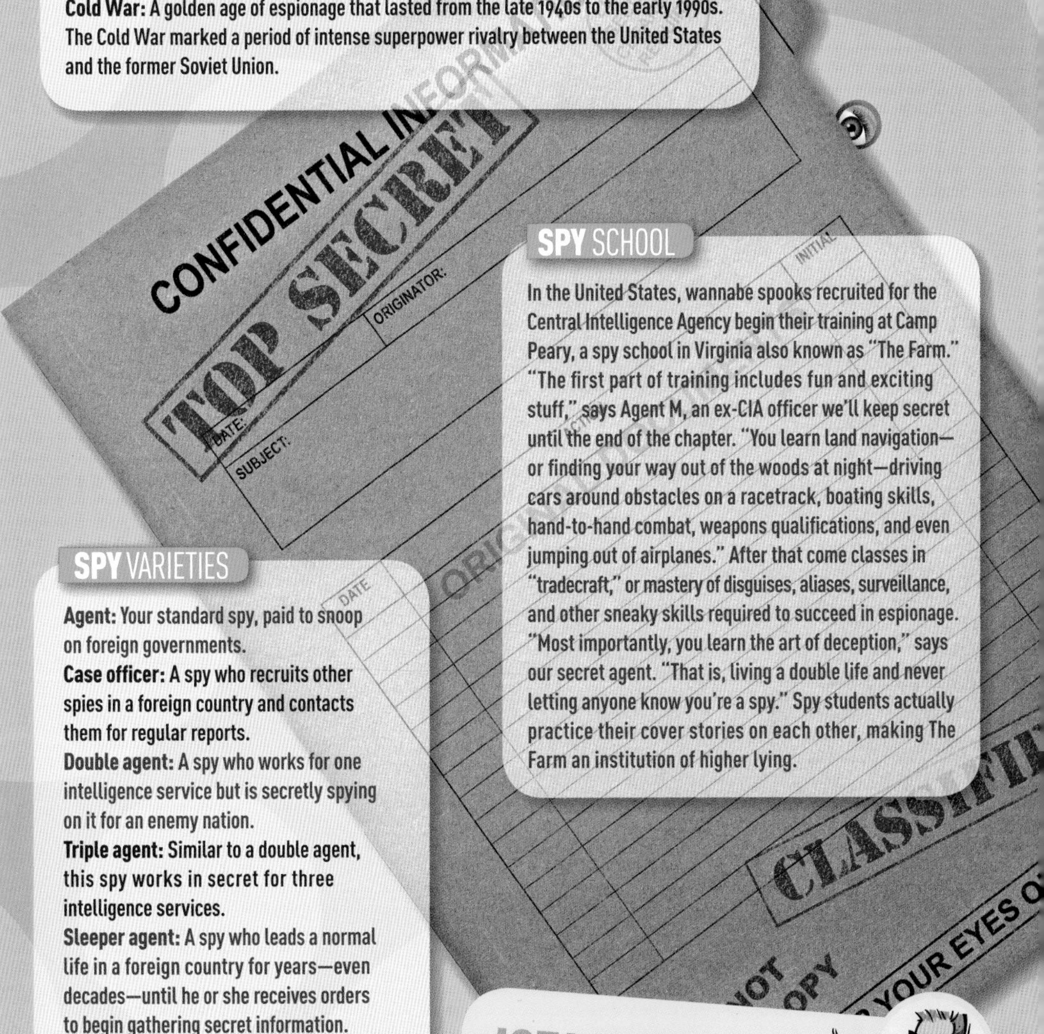

ESSENTIAL ESPIONAGE TERMS

Legend: A spy's cover story while in the field. It's a big bogus identity that includes a phony name, job, and family background. If a spy's legend is discovered as a lie, his or her "cover is blown" or "compromised."

Infiltrate: To slip into a place undetected for the purpose of spying.

Exfiltrate: To leave that place without getting caught, typically after your cover is blown.

Cold War: A golden age of espionage that lasted from the late 1940s to the early 1990s. The Cold War marked a period of intense superpower rivalry between the United States and the former Soviet Union.

CONFIDENTIAL INFORMATION

TOP SECRET

ORIGINATOR:

DATE:

SUBJECT:

SPY SCHOOL

In the United States, wannabe spooks recruited for the Central Intelligence Agency begin their training at Camp Peary, a spy school in Virginia also known as "The Farm." "The first part of training includes fun and exciting stuff," says Agent M, an ex-CIA officer we'll keep secret until the end of the chapter. "You learn land navigation—or finding your way out of the woods at night—driving cars around obstacles on a racetrack, boating skills, hand-to-hand combat, weapons qualifications, and even jumping out of airplanes." After that come classes in "tradecraft," or mastery of disguises, aliases, surveillance, and other sneaky skills required to succeed in espionage. "Most importantly, you learn the art of deception," says our secret agent. "That is, living a double life and never letting anyone know you're a spy." Spy students actually practice their cover stories on each other, making The Farm an institution of higher lying.

SPY VARIETIES

Agent: Your standard spy, paid to snoop on foreign governments.

Case officer: A spy who recruits other spies in a foreign country and contacts them for regular reports.

Double agent: A spy who works for one intelligence service but is secretly spying on it for an enemy nation.

Triple agent: Similar to a double agent, this spy works in secret for three intelligence services.

Sleeper agent: A spy who leads a normal life in a foreign country for years—even decades—until he or she receives orders to begin gathering secret information.

Analyst: Not a spy in the traditional sense, analysts gather information from afar by scouring public sources (newspapers, websites, and TV news), or they listen in on phone calls and secretly read emails. In the U.S., analysts work for the National Security Agency to monitor "signals intelligence."

CLASSIFIED

NOT COPY

FOR YOUR EYES O

'STACHE'S SECRET

A team of marine biologists in Massachusetts, U.S.A., has figured out how to control a shark by fitting electrodes that stimulate the smell centers of its brain. The military may use these remote-control sharks as underwater spies.

SPY SURVIVAL GUIDE

Imagine moving to a country far from home, having to speak fluently in a foreign language, and trying to convince everyone you meet that you're someone you're not. You might spend your days at a phony job, but your real career is to swipe secrets or convince others to steal them for you. Oh, and you'll suffer a horrible punishment if anyone discovers your true identity. Welcome to clandestine operations, where sneakiness is key to survival. Intelligent espionage agents limit their risk with these time-tested rules of tradecraft.

CLANDESTINE DOS AND DON'TS

DO

Make sure you haven't been followed. "Whenever we go to meetings, we conduct what's called a surveillance-detection route," says Agent M, our ex-CIA officer you'll meet at the end of the chapter. "This means walking or driving around and trying to determine if people or cars are following you." One technique is to make only left turns at intersections and see if anyone follows you.

DON'T

Break character or do anything unusual. Aldrich Ames, a CIA case officer working as a double agent for the former Soviet Union, got caught after he began buying jewelry, fancy cars, and an expensive house he couldn't afford on his CIA salary.

DO

Use dead drops, or predetermined spots for passing items (secret photos, documents, cash payments, etc.) between spies without them having to meet. The best dead drops blend in with the background—trash cans, shrubbery, even doggie doo (fast-forward to the gadgets section for the icky details).

DON'T

Trust anyone. "People may not be who they are or what they seem," says Agent M. "Circumstances change rapidly. You have to be able to adapt in a few minutes—or seconds."

DON'T

Admit to anything if you're caught. "Even if your cover is seemingly blown," says Agent M, "you should continue to deny, deny, deny any involvement with the CIA or spying."

DO

Stick to the Moscow Rules, a set of common-sense guidelines laid out for secret agents who worked in Moscow, dangerous territory for foreign spies during the Cold War.

RULES INCLUDE . . .

1) Never assume anything.
2) If something feels wrong, it probably is.
3) Go with the flow.
4) Always have backup options ready.
5) Choose your own time and place to act.
6) Never get cocky or taunt your enemies.

DON'T

Let your guard down or feel like your old self. Being a spy is a full-time job, and you can't take the weekends off from your secret identity. "I would never reveal too much about myself," says Agent M, "even to other Americans, colleagues, or friends."

DO

Develop your powers of observation and memory. You won't always have access to a spy camera or photocopier for swiping secret documents. Sometimes you'll need to "take a photo with your eyes" and memorize important details to write down once you get alone time.

THE Limping LADY

WORLD WAR II'S "MOST DANGEROUS" SPY

VIRGINIA HALL NEEDED A DISGUISE, AND NOT JUST FOR HER FACE. SHE WAS AN AMERICAN SPY DEEP IN ENEMY TERRITORY— NAZI-OCCUPIED FRANCE—IN 1944. The Nazis' secret police were hot on her trail. "We must find and destroy her," their ruthless orders read. "She is the most dangerous of all Allied spies." Wanted posters described a dark-haired "woman with a limp." Changing her hair color would be easy, but Hall—who had lost her left leg below the knee in a hunting accident before the war—would have to do something about that limp, a dead giveaway.

Born in Maryland in 1906 to a wealthy family, Hall attended the most prestigious colleges and excelled at learning languages. She longed to be a diplomat, to travel Europe as a representative of the United States. Her hunting accident put an end to that promising career. But when World War II erupted in Europe, Hall found a new calling: espionage.

She volunteered for Britain's secret intelligence agency, becoming its first female operative dispatched to the German-occupied part of France. Hall spent 15 months organizing the French resistance under the cover story of an American reporter. When all of France fell to the Germans in 1942, she had to get out of the country fast—or risk execution as a spy. Slowed but not stopped by her artificial leg (which she nicknamed "Cuthbert"), Hall escaped over the rugged Pyrenees mountains on foot.

Now a seasoned spy, Hall had no trouble finding work with the U.S. Office of Strategic Services (the OSS), which later became the Central Intelligence Agency. Her mission: Return to France and report on the German army's every move. "Cuthbert" kept her from parachuting behind enemy lines, so Hall hitched a ride on a British PT boat. She helped sneak weapons to Allied commandos and trained French resistance fighters to sabotage bridges, trains, and power lines. Using a pedal-powered radio hidden in a suitcase, Hall broadcast regular reports on German activity, becoming the most despised Allied spy in France. The hunt for the "limping lady" was on.

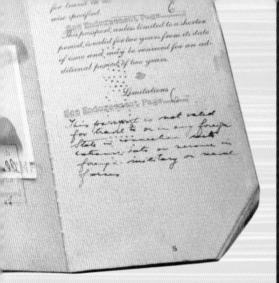

Hall put together the perfect disguise: that of an old milkmaid. She dyed her hair gray, slipped into heavy skirts to hide her thin frame, and shuffled her feet to disguise her limp. She sold cheese and milk in villages right under the noses of the Germans, monitoring their movements. She broadcast from different attics and barns so enemies could never lock down her signal. Hall remained one step ahead of the Nazis until Allied troops relieved her and her band of rebels.

After the war, both the British and U.S. intelligence agencies hailed Hall as a hero, but the master spy insisted on keeping a low profile. U.S. President Harry Truman wanted to award her the Distinguished Service Cross for her bravery; she requested that the founder of the OSS give it to her in a private ceremony. Hall joined the CIA in 1951 and stayed there for the rest of her career. "She was an amazing and brave woman," says Agent M, "and an incredible spy."

MORE MASTER SPIES

MARY BOWSER posed as an illiterate slave to spy on the Confederate White House during the U.S. Civil War. Highly educated, she was able to read and memorize any important documents she came across.

CAPTAIN NATHAN HALE volunteered to spy on the British during the Revolutionary War. America's first espionage agent, Hale is famous for his final words after he was caught and hanged by the British: "I only regret that I have but one life to give for my country."

JOHN ANTHONY WALKER used his position as a communications specialist in the U.S. Navy to obtain plans for secret submarine technology and sell them to the former Soviet Union. By the time he was caught in 1985, Walker had recruited family members into his espionage business and sold enough secrets to give the Soviet Union an edge in the Cold War.

SPIES IN THE SKIES

RECONNAISSANCE SATELLITES PLAY PEEK-A-BOO FROM SPACE

NEXT TIME YOU STEP OUTSIDE, LOOK UP AND SAY "CHEESE." SOMEONE MIGHT BE TAKING YOUR PICTURE! Constellations of imaging satellites swarm the heavens, snapping high-definition photos of the terrain far below for scientists, city planners, mapmakers, government agencies, and the web-based virtual globe of Google Earth. But while most of these eagle-eyed "birds" are easy to track on websites (and even an app for your smartphone), an elusive few soar in secret to snoop on various countries from low Earth orbit. We track the telemetry of these sneaky spacecraft...

CORONA PROGRAM LAUNCHED IN: 1959   DECLASSIFIED

Built at the beginning of America's space program, the Corona series of spy satellites was so top secret that even its code name had a code name: "Discoverer." As far as the public knew, the Discoverer payloads included probes, primates, and experiments essential to planning human exploration of outer space. Instead, each craft carried two nine-foot (2.7-m)-long cameras and up to six miles (9.7 km) of film. Nearly 150 Corona satellites were launched to spy on the former Soviet Union and the People's Republic of China in the 1960s.

Recovering pictures from orbit wasn't easy in the days before digital photography and wireless downloading. Each finished roll of Corona film ejected from the satellite aboard a tiny capsule shielded to survive the fiery reentry into Earth's atmosphere. Air Force planes trailing long hooks caught the parachute-equipped capsules in midair over the Pacific Ocean—before they could fall into enemy hands.

SPY-PHOTO QUALITY: Corona cameras could reveal structures down to 40 feet (12.2 m).

HEXAGON PROGRAM LAUNCHED IN: 1971 DECLASSIFIED

Nicknamed "Big Birds" (each satellite was the size of a bus), Hexagon spacecraft were an upgrade from the Corona satellites, equipped with powerful cameras that captured larger patches of terrain at much greater resolution. By the time the last of the Big Birds rocketed into orbit in 1986, they had photographed the entire surface of the Earth. These craft ejected their film in capsules just like the Corona satellites. When one capsule's parachute failed to open on reentry in 1971, the U.S. Navy sent its deepest-diving submarine to recover the film from three miles (4.8 km) down in the Pacific Ocean.

SPY-PHOTO QUALITY: Hexagon cameras could resolve details down to two feet (0.6 m), such as home base in a baseball field.

ORION PROGRAM LAUNCHED IN: 1995

Reconnaissance satellites are more than just eyes in the sky for spy agencies. They're their "ears," too! The Orion satellites carry enormous radio dishes that gather signals intelligence—or electronic signals such as radar, radio waves, and telecommunication traffic. In other words, these sneaky satellites can eavesdrop on your phone calls!

CLASSIFIED

KENNAN PROGRAM LAUNCHED IN: 1976 CLASSIFIED

Although the Corona and Hexagon satellites gave the United States valuable sneak peeks at its rivals, both systems suffered from one major flaw: They were useless once they ran out of film. (Considering each satellite cost hundreds of millions of dollars to build and launch, these were the world's most expensive disposable cameras!) The top-secret Kennan satellites—still in use and classified to this day—solved this problem. They were reportedly the first satellites that carried digital cameras, and they could broadcast their images live through a top secret network of communication satellites. They're the closest equivalent to the high-tech monitoring systems seen in spy movies.

SPY-PHOTO QUALITY: Kennan cameras can reportedly resolve details as small as the digits on a license plate.

'STACHE'S SECRET

When spy agencies and the military need eyes in the sky but don't have time to reposition a spy satellite, they send in the drones. Unmanned aerial vehicles (UAVs) are small aircraft that carry cameras and sensors instead of pilots and crew. They're flown by remote control from anywhere in the world—or even by automatic pilot. They've become a popular snooping tool in clandestine operations, which have changed drastically since the days of the Cold War.

105

REAL-LIFE SPY

JAMES BOND MIGHT HAVE HIS POISON-PROPELLING PEN AND LASER WRISTWATCH, BUT REAL-LIFE SPIES WIELD WILD GADGETS, TOO. With the help of the International Spy Museum in Washington, D.C., we gathered ten of the coolest, cruelest, sneakiest spy tools, many of which you can see at the museum.

LIPSTICK PISTOL CIRCA 1965

Wielded by female agents of the former Soviet Union's espionage agency during the Cold War, this little lip-gloss canister hid a big surprise: a 4.5-mm single-shot pistol. "It delivered the ultimate 'kiss of death,'" says Peter Earnest, the International Spy Museum's executive director and a 36-year career CIA operations officer. Agents fired the mini-pistol by twisting the tube—the same motion that extends the gloss in a regular lipstick applicator. You wouldn't want to forget this gizmo in your makeup bag!

MINOX CAMERA CIRCA 1960 TO TODAY

A savvy spy's hidden camera of choice for half a century, the Minox could snap 50 pictures on a single roll, and its special lens captured the tiniest details, such as the fine print in classified documents. It was a favorite of John Walker to document America's military secrets. The camera is still made today, although it doesn't see nearly as much espionage action as in the days of the Cold War.

CONTINUED ON THE NEXT PAGE

GADGETS

BUTTONHOLE CAMERA CIRCA 1970
The lens of this tiny camera was tucked behind the right middle button of an ordinary coat, perfectly positioned for photographing unsuspecting subjects. Snapping a picture was easy: The coat's wearer squeezed a shutter cable hidden in the coat pocket, which caused the fake button to open and snap a picture. Several types of buttonhole cameras were widely used in the former Soviet Union, Europe, and North America.

"THE THING" CIRCA 1950s
The U.S. ambassador to Russia was delighted when Soviet school-children gave him this hand-carved wooden replica of the Great Seal of the United States in 1946. Told it represented friendship between the two nations, he displayed it proudly in his Moscow study for years. But less than a decade later, technicians discovered that the seal came with a bonus gift: a small wireless listening device—called a bug in spy speak. The microphone was impossible to detect when activated by a beam generated from a van parked nearby. It didn't require wires or even batteries—just air to fill the surrounding cavities, supplied by a tiny hole in the eagle's beak. The seal was code-named "The Thing" because no one knew what else to call it.

DOO-DOO TRANSMITTER CIRCA 1970
When agents and soldiers behind enemy lines needed to hide homing beacons to direct aerial reconnaissance, the Central Intelligence Agency came up with this disgusting disguise. Radio transmitters and "dead-drop" canisters (used to pass secret messages) were camouflaged as convincing chunks of poop, something no enemies would investigate or touch.

UMBRELLA DART-GUN CIRCA 1978

This umbrella fired a BB-size pellet coated in a deadly poison, which only needed to break the skin to kill. A Bulgarian agent used such an umbrella to assassinate enemy-of-the-state Georgi Markov, who recalled being shot by such a device before falling ill and dying the next day.

PIGEON CAMERA CIRCA 1918

You've heard of carrier pigeons? How about pigeon spies! Before reconnaissance planes and surveillance satellites, intelligence offices outfitted pigeons with tiny cameras and released them over military sites. As the birds flew, the cameras continuously clicked away, snapping pictures that were developed and scrutinized for intel when the pigeons reached their destination.

SHOE PHONE CIRCA 1960s

A shoe that doubles as a telephone is a famous funny gadget in spy fiction, but the shoe transmitter is more of a sneaky "gift" than a gag. Romanian secret agents installed a microphone and transmitter in the heel of a foreign diplomat's shoes that he ordered though the mail. The diplomat didn't know he was bugged until technicians discovered a radio signal coming from his feet.

TREE TRANSMITTER CIRCA 1970

CIA agents planted this solar-powered eavesdropping gizmo in the woods near Moscow, where it intercepted radio signals from a nearby Soviet missile system and transmitted the data via satellite to the United States. Despite its clever disguise in a phony tree stump (with a transparent top for the solar panels), the bug was eventually discovered by KGB agents.

POISON-PILL GLASSES CIRCA 1975

A gadget of last resort, these thick-framed glasses contained a tiny cyanide pill in the arm that desperate agents could swallow if they preferred death to capture. Agents could also chew the arm of the glasses to eat the poison pill without raising suspicion.

'STACHE'S SECRET

The lipstick pistol and umbrella dart-launcher are just two of the many guns hidden in everyday objects. Spies packed pistols disguised as pens, watches, flashlights, rings, cigarette cases, gloves—enough lethal objects to fill a department store.

Fringe Elements

THE SPOOKY SCIENCE OF SPOOKS

BUG OFF

Listening devices come in all shapes and sizes—as big as a fist and as itty-bitty as a pencil eraser—but the Insectocopter was in a class by itself. It was a bug that laid other bugs! The CIA tried to develop this robotic dragonfly in the 1970s to drop listening devices by remote control. The Insectocopter buzzed wildly out of control in crosswinds, though, so the project never really got off the ground.

MIND OVER MATTER

A girl named Nina Kulagina noticed she could make things move when she got mad while growing up in the former Soviet Union, and officials in the government took notice. They believed Kulagina might have the power of telekinesis, the flexing of mental muscles to move objects in the real world (sort of like the Force in Star Wars). Soviet officials videotaped her shoving objects on tables and plucking single matchsticks from piles of them with her mind. The Soviets hoped to develop telekinesis to disrupt the guidance systems of enemy nuclear missiles. Skeptics think she faked these feats through magician's sleight of hand.

SEEING THINGS

The United States wasn't about to sit back and let its Soviet rivals win the psychic arms race, so the Central Intelligence Agency conducted its own research into "paranormal phenomena" beginning in 1972. As part of its top secret Star Gate project, the CIA studied clairvoyance: the ability to mentally visualize people, objects, or events that are somewhere else—even on the other side of the world! The CIA hoped to use psychic spies for mental missions, such as peeking at military bases in other countries and assisting with hostage rescues. The program was shut down in 1995, despite some promising results in the laboratory.

TRUTH BE TOLD

Squeezing information from bad guys in spy movies is easy: Just inject them with a special serum and they'll tell nothing but the truth. But although such a substance—called sodium pentothal—really does exist and has reportedly been used in CIA interrogations, it's not the all-powerful "truth serum" portrayed in films. Such substances simply make the subject more talkative and less inhibited about what he or she is saying. Serum swallowers might blab for hours, but what they say is likely all nonsense.

THINKING OUT LOUD

The Soviets were interested in more than just telekinesis. Beginning as early as the 1920s at Leningrad's Institute for Brain Research, they began studying all sorts of "extrasensory perception." Chief among them was telepathy, the ability to receive the thoughts of others and send mental messages in return. Soviet scientists hoped they could use telepathy to communicate with submarines without relying on radio gear.

Eye-to-Eye With a SPY

YOU'VE HEARD FROM THE MYSTERIOUS "AGENT M" THROUGHOUT THIS CHAPTER. **Now she's finally ready to step from the shadows.** Meet Lindsay Moran, a "case officer" for the Central Intelligence Agency from 1998 to 2003. After completing her training at "The Farm" CIA spy school in Virginia, she was dispatched to the Republic of Macedonia to gather intelligence and recruit other spies. Now an author, Officer Moran has arranged a meeting with Agent 'Stache to spill her top secrets of the spying profession...

Agent 'Stache: My dossier on you—actually, your book, *Blowing My Cover: My Life as a CIA Spy*—says you started spying early. What got you into espionage as a kid?
Moran: I was obsessed with a series of books about a character named Harriet the Spy. Also, whenever I got in trouble and was sent to my room for a "time-out," I would spy on the neighbors and anyone outside. I also communicated in secret code using flashlights with my best friend who lived next door.

Agent 'Stache: What skills should junior spies focus on?
Moran: You should do well in school, because it's very difficult to get into the CIA. Learning other languages is also helpful, especially difficult languages that not many Americans know—like Chinese or Arabic. It's good to know what is going on in the world. But you can start with geography, so you'll know where you are going when you are sent on your first mission.

Agent 'Stache: You went to Harvard and won an elite scholarship. Are all spies as smart as you?
Moran: You don't have to go to Harvard to be a good spy. In fact, the most important attribute is something we call "street smarts"—or being able to think and act quickly, especially in the face of danger.

Agent 'Stache: You became a "case officer" for the CIA. Is that the same thing as a secret agent?
Moran: As "case officers" or "operations officers," we don't call ourselves spies or secret agents. But that's in fact what we were, living undercover in foreign countries and "stealing" secrets!

Agent 'Stache: Did you have a cover story?
Moran: Yes. Mine was that of a "diplomat," which is someone who represents their home country overseas. It was good cover because it gave me a lot of access to "targets": people that the U.S. government is interested in.

Agent 'Stache: So you recruited others to be spies. What did you look for?
Moran: I looked for people whom I could convince it was in their best interest to give me secrets. Sometimes, they really liked the United States. Other times, they just needed or wanted money. We typically pay our foreign sources of information as a reward for giving us secrets.

Agent 'Stache: Ever accidentally recruit a double agent? How about a triple one?
Moran: Not that I know of! But keeping your agents straight—and especially remembering where and when you are supposed to meet them—is one of the challenges of being a spy.

SECRET AGENT 'STACHE
TRACKS DOWN
A REAL-LIFE AGENT
OF ESPIONAGE

Agent 'Stache: **Was it hard to keep up your cover all the time?**
Moran: I never really felt like I was myself, even if I was using my real name—as I did when I wasn't "operational." You tend to become a bit paranoid.

Agent 'Stache: **Do spy skills come in handy in everyday life?**
Moran: I am a much better driver because of the "defensive driving" training: a weeklong CIA course affectionately called "Crash and Burn."

Agent 'Stache: **Movie spies can hurl bad guys through windows with just their pinky fingers. Can you do that?**
Moran: I wish that I could, but my instincts—and spy training—would tell me to escape rather than try to fight with my pinky. I am good at kicking bad guys in the shin. They actually taught us to do that at CIA.

Agent 'Stache: **What are some other differences between make-believe spies and real ones?**
Moran: Make-believe spies always have a cool gadget on hand to get them out of tough situations. Real spies more often have to talk their way out of it.

Agent 'Stache: **Is being a spy a lonely job?**
Moran: Yes, it was very lonely. I couldn't tell anyone where I was working or what I was doing. The only people who knew I was at CIA were my mother, father, and brother. But all they knew was that they could not tell anyone that. They didn't know what I was doing. That's the nature of being a spy, and I decided I didn't want to spend the rest of my life living that way. But many people do.

OUT OF THE SHADOWS:
Former CIA spy Lindsay Moran relied on training and instincts instead of gadgets.

Agent 'Stache: **Hey, how do I know you really left the CIA? Maybe this is all part of your new cover!**
Moran: Now you're thinking like a real spy!

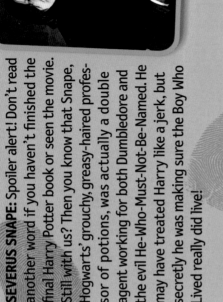

SEVERUS SNAPE: Spoiler alert! Don't read another word if you haven't finished the final Harry Potter book or seen the movie. Still with us? Then you know that Snape, Hogwarts' grouchy, greasy-haired professor of potions, was actually a double agent working for both Dumbledore and the evil He-Who-Must-Not-Be-Named. He may have treated Harry like a jerk, but secretly he was making sure the Boy Who Lived really did live!

SPY KIDS: Teenage siblings Carmen and Juni Cortez take the easy route into international espionage—they're born into it. When they discover that their parents are retired spies and have been kidnapped by an archcriminal, the Cortez kids convince their kooky uncle to supply them with all sorts of nifty spy gadgets to mount a rescue—and save the world. After succeeding in their mission, the spy kids join the family business in the OSS (Organization of Super Spies).

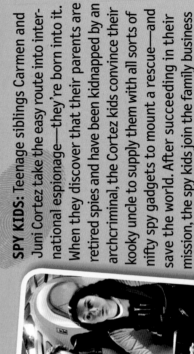

007: If you're unfamiliar with this British superspy, you've obviously never heard him make his trademark introduction: "The name's Bond, James Bond." Since he was created in 1953 by author Ian Fleming, Agent 007 has saved the world in more than 20 films and at least twice as many novels.

Along the way, this agent in "Her Majesty's secret service" laid the ground rules for all pop-culture spooks: They're snarky, suave, and wield the coolest secret gadgets—from laser-firing watches to cars that quick-change into submarines.

CLASSIFIED Information

SHHH SCALE

SPECTRUM OF HUSH–HUSH HIERARCHY

SUPREMELY SNEAKY

DEFINITELY DEVIOUS

SOLIDLY STEALTHY

SLIGHTLY SHIFTY

Orion Satellite

Insectocopter

Doo-Doo Transmitter

Buttonhole Camera

Lipstick Pistol

Secret Agent 'Stache Ranks **ESPIONAGE EQUIPMENT**

CHAPTER 6

Mystery Spots

FINDING PIRATE TREASURE AND LONG-LOST RUINS IS EASY IN BOOKS AND MOVIES. X MARKS THE SPOT!

But secret sites in the real world are never that easy to uncover. Archaeologists must piece together myths, historical records, and scraps of maps to pinpoint important ancient places. Trapdoors lock away priceless treasures and very important people. But what history has hidden away, you get to uncover in this chapter on secret spaces and peek-a-boo places. Get ready to wander off the map . . .

THE HOLE TRUTH

HISTORY'S DEEP, DARK SECRETS

SECRET CELLS

Medieval castles didn't have dungeons (which evolved from the word "donjon," the original name for towering keeps). Lords, ladies, and knights captured in battle were held in the donjon's uppermost floors until their ransoms were paid. But some castles did have secret rooms called oubliettes—accessible via a trapdoor high in the ceiling—where a castle lord's most hated enemies would be left and forgotten.

ESCAPE ROUTES

Hidden passages had many purposes (in more modern structures, they were used to spy on guests through the walls), but in cathedrals and castles they typically served as a means of emergency escape. Medieval castles in particular often had secret exits—called sally ports—that led to underground tunnels. Defenders in a siege could sneak in supplies or launch surprise counterattacks.

HISTORY IS FULL OF HOLES: PRIEST HOLES, MURDER HOLES, HIDDEN TUNNELS, and other undercover chambers of secrets, accessible only by elaborate trapdoors and passwords. Stealthy construction crews installed such hideaways for all sorts of sneaky reasons, from stashing treasure to protecting people. Explore them yourself as we unearth six kinds of undercover architecture ...

HOLY HOLES

England's Catholics came under siege starting in the reign of Queen Elizabeth I in 1558. Declared outlaws, priests fled churches and sought safety within the homes of their followers, who built "priest holes" to hide the clergy from authorities.

CONFOUNDING CORRIDORS

Ancient Egyptians built dead-end hallways and decoy treasure rooms in their towering tombs to throw off grave robbers. Japanese warlords commissioned similar twisting hallways to confuse and corner would-be assassins. In modern times, construction on the Winchester Mystery House in San Jose, California, U.S.A., continued around the clock for decades, resulting in a maze of twisting hallways, stairways to nowhere, dead-end doors, and secret passages. The wealthy widow who lived there hoped to confuse the mansion's resident ghosts.

MURDER HOLES

These secret recesses pitted the vaulted ceiling above a castle's gatehouse, letting defenders on the floor above fire arrows and dump boiling water and scalding sand on attackers who breached the gate.

WAR ROOMS

Hidden quarters save lives and accommodate spies in times of war. Jewish refugees, for instance, hid from the Nazis in blocked-off attics and secret rooms before and during World War II. Anne Frank and her family famously sought refuge in a secret Amsterdam apartment hidden behind a bookcase. A group of student roommates in Norway, meanwhile, recently discovered a secret attic chamber full of maps and messages. It turns out the room was used to print anti-Nazi newspapers during World War II.

WHAT ON EARTH?

FIVE FAR-OUT GEOGRAPHICAL FEATURES YOU CAN SEE ONLY FROM HIGH IN THE SKY

HEART LAND

The owner of this tiny island off the coast of Croatia was clueless when couples started contacting him with requests to visit on Valentine's Day—until he took a bird's-eye view of the property from Google Earth, a web program that connects satellite imagery to create a complete picture of the planet. Turns out the island had a distinctly romantic shape. The isle has since been renamed Lover's Island and is a popular destination among honeymooners and the heartsick.

COLOSSAL COLONEL

Most billboards catch your attention from the highway or sidewalk, but one fried-chicken chain created an oversize logo visible only from an airplane. KFC founder Colonel Sanders is rendered in 65,000 red-and-white tiles arrayed across an 87,000-square-foot (8,082-sq-m) patch of Nevada desert, not far from the mysterious Air Force base Area 51. It's not even the only advertisement you can see from 30,000 feet (9,144 m). Similar sprawling signs were created for the Coca-Cola and Firefox Internet browser logos in far-flung parts of the world.

HERE'S WALDO

Call off the search. Waldo has been found. The lanky, bespectacled wanderer who so famously lost himself in the crowd in his series of Where's Waldo? activity books has turned up on Google Earth. A Canadian artist painted a 55-foot (16.8-m)-tall likeness of Waldo on a Vancouver roof. She inspired other artists to replicate supersize Waldos on rooftops across the globe, making a game out of spotting the strolling giant on Google Earth.

SWEET PRINTS

The name of the "Fingermaze"—a squiggly labyrinth of stone set in the turf in a rural English park—doesn't make much sense until you see it from high above. It looks like a giant fingerprint!

SPACEY PLACE

The practice of creating ground-bound images for sky-high viewing is nothing new. Sixteen hundred years ago, the people of Peru's ancient Nazca culture traced titanic animals, runway-size rectangles, and abstract shapes larger than football fields on the floor of a desert plateau. Some flying-saucer enthusiasts believe the figures—some of which look like landing strips—were created for ancient visitors from other planets.

INSIDE OUT

HOUSES With Something to HIDE

SECRET CHAMBERS ARE NO LONGER THE DOMAIN OF MEDIEVAL CASTLE LORDS AND SCOOBY DOO VILLAINS. More and more ordinary homeowners are stashing hidden rooms in their houses. They're camouflaging the doors with bookshelves, stairways, wooden paneling, brick walls—all custom-built entrances that open only to those who press the hidden button or know the secret knock. Prices for disguised doors range from $800 up to $25,000 for deluxe motorized models that look straight out of a Bond villain's volcano lair.

Although many of these chambers function as "panic rooms" featuring reinforced walls and heavy locks that keep occupants safe from potential home invaders, just as many are built for the fun of it. "I was inspired by a trapdoor in (the video game) *Resident Evil,*" says David S. J. Hodgson, a writer who installed a secret room (he calls it his oubliette) in his house in Camas, Washington, U.S.A. Press the hidden button in Hodgson's study and a bookcase swings open to reveal stairs leading down to a home theater complete with a pool table, library, and gargoyles from medieval English churches. Scan these pages to spy more secret rooms exposed...

OUTSIDE IN:
THREE
CAMOUFLAGED
HOUSES

'STACHE'S SECRET

Camouflage isn't just for casas. Los Angeles artist Joshua Callaghan hid the city's unsightly utility boxes by wrapping them in digital photos of the background.

WOOD HOUSE This structure in the Netherlands looks like a tidy stack of logs—until the occupants open the windows. Ta-da! It's actually a recording studio built to blend into the woodsy background.

DUNE HOUSE A house any Hobbit would love, this beachside duplex in Florida, U.S.A., was buried in the sand so it wouldn't block the neighbor's view. Despite its low profile, the Dune House offers dramatic vistas of the Atlantic through two large windows.

STONE HOUSE The Casa de Penedo, or "House of Stone," in Portugal's Fafe Mountains was built from four boulders. Despite its Stone Age design, this cozy abode features a fireplace and even a swimming pool!

SUNKEN TREASURE

ARCHAEOLOGIST UNCOVERS A LOST EGYPTIAN CITY

IT WAS A CITY OF GODS AND GOLD, A VIBRANT PORT ON THE MEDITERRANEAN, BUSTLING WITH BOLD TRADERS FROM ACROSS THE ANCIENT WORLD. Known as Thonis to the Egyptians and Heracleion to the Greeks, this harbor town was the gateway to ancient Egypt. Egyptians worshiped the ram-headed god Amun in a titanic stone temple, also home to a shrine to the Greek hero Heracles. Well-to-do merchants sold jewelry in the shadow of colossal statues and walls inscribed with hieroglyphics.

Then disaster struck! Earthquakes and floods wracked Thonis-Heracleion. It was swallowed by the sea in the eighth century A.D., sinking into legend. Outside of the writings of Herodotus, a fifth-century B.C. Greek historian, archaeologists found few traces that the city ever existed. It became nothing more than a footnote in the myth of Helen of Troy, the world's most beautiful woman, who visited the city with Paris, her Trojan love.

But Thonis-Heracleion emerged from mythology into reality in 2000, when French marine archaeologist Franck Goddio, through systematic underwater mapping, found the lost city on the bottom of Aboukir Bay near Alexandria, Egypt. (Goddio had previously discovered the sunken city of Canopus nearby.) He uncovered statues of Egyptian gods, followed by richly inscribed pillars, temple walls, and more than 60 ancient shipwrecks. The port of Thonis-Heracleion was no longer lost. Here it was, frozen in time and preserved in sand, just 30 feet (9.1 m) underwater.

A TALE OF TWO
SECRET CITIES

THE LAS VEGAS TUNNELS

More than 300 miles (483 km) of storm drains criss-cross beneath the neon-lit streets of Las Vegas, Nevada, U.S.A. Here, beneath the casinos and luxury hotels, drifters down on their luck created a hidden city. Dark, damp chambers have become underground art galleries and living spaces, complete with beds, couches, and other homey touches.

CAMP CENTURY

In 1960, the U.S. military built a nuclear-powered base under the Greenland ice 800 miles (1,288 km) south of the North Pole. Called Camp Century, it was more like a subterranean city, with 21 tunnels connecting living quarters to a theater, library, barbershop, laboratories, and more. The military claimed Camp Century was just a research base for studying the Arctic ice, but the project was actually a test run for a secret missile-launching facility. Those plans were scrapped after shifting glacial ice slowly crushed the base. It was abandoned for good in 1969.

LOST OR FOUND

TRACKING DOWN LOST SITES

LOST

ATLANTIS

The Greek philosopher Plato described Atlantis as a powerful island civilization that sunk into the Atlantic Ocean long ago. When divers discovered the strange undersea rock formation known as Bimini Road in the Bahamas, they wondered if they'd found Atlantis. Geologists say no, and Atlantis remains an alluring legend.

FOUND

ABANDONED SUBWAY STOPS

One of the world's oldest subway systems, New York City's sprawling network of underground tracks contains more than 15 decommissioned stops that sit like ghost stations under the busy streets. Some have been preserved for tours (such as the stunning, cathedral-like City Hall stop on the 6 train) while others can only be glimpsed by riders who know when and where to look out the window on their daily commute.

AMBER ROOM

Built in the early 18th century in Prussia, this priceless piece of architecture was assembled from sculpted panels of amber set against gold and mirrors. It moved from palace to palace before disappearing in World War II (some believe it was destroyed by bombs; others think it was hidden in a bunker or a long-lost mine). The room has since been re-created in Catherine Palace in St. Petersburg, Russia, but the original is still lost to time.

CATACOMBS OF PARIS

The City of Light sits above a realm of darkness, a never-ending labyrinth of sewers, vaults, wine cellars, canals, quarries, and—famously—crypts. In 1785, workers began exhuming corpses from overflowing cemeteries and dumping them into the city's limestone quarries. Six million skeletons were relocated to these catacombs in just 30 years! Today, the tombs are a top tourist attraction, but exploring too deeply into this underground realm is against the law. That doesn't stop adventurous "cataphiles" from creeping into the darkness through secret doorways and unmarked manholes.

EL DORADO

When the Spanish conquistadors explored South America in the early 16th century, they heard tantalizing tales of a gilded city founded by a king coated in gold dust. They called the chief "El Dorado," or "the gilded one," and they believed his city was the source of all the gold in the New World. The conquistadors thought they were closing in on El Dorado when they found gold at the bottom of Colombia's Lake Guatavita in 1545, but the trail ended there. Tales of this fabled "city of gold" have since lured many explorers to their deaths.

'STACHE'S SECRET

Despite what you've seen in timber-shivering pirate flicks, buccaneers didn't bury their treasure or mark its location with a big X on a cloth map.

SNEAKY DESTINATIONS

TAKE A STEALTHY SPIN TO THESE MYSTERY SPOTS

PART ONE: THE UNITED STATES

INTERNATIONAL SPY MUSEUM
Washington, D.C.

Learn the art of espionage and inspect high-tech spy gizmos—including the lipstick pistol, buttonhole camera, and invisible ink—at this museum dedicated to clandestine operations. The Operation Spy adventure has you decrypting secret transmissions, infiltrating and escaping a secure facility, and interrogating an enemy agent—all in less than an hour.

KORNER'S FOLLY
Kernersville, North Carolina

Billed as the "strangest house in the world," this rambling mansion features secret underground passages, tiny rooms, trapdoors, and hidden compartments, all built to the eccentric specifications of Jules Gilmer Korner in 1880. Rumor has it an acquaintance told Gilmer that his house was a folly, which tickled Gilmer so much that he had the name set in a plaque outside. Today, you can tour the house and decide if it was folly or just fun.

OREGON VORTEX
Gold Hill, Oregon

Balls roll uphill, chairs sit on walls, and people look taller or shorter depending on where they stand at this topsy-turvy attraction and "House of Mystery" in Oregon's gold-mining country. The Vortex's guides claim a whirlpool of invisible energy is behind the strange goings-on; scientists will tell you it's all an optical illusion. Regardless, the Oregon Vortex is a fun place to visit and one of more than a dozen "Mystery Spots," "Gravity Hills," and similarly physics-bending attractions spread across the country.

GREENBRIER BUNKER
White Sulfur Springs, West Virginia

Until 1992, no one without the proper security clearance knew about a nuke-proof bunker beneath the Greenbrier luxury resort in West Virginia. Given the code name "Project Greek Island" and stocked with enough food to last 30 years, it was a top secret underground refuge for members of Congress in the event of World War III. Now declassified and open for tours, the bunker stands as a fascinating monument to the Cold War.

SINGER CASTLE
Dark Island, New York

You'd expect that a castle built on a rock called Dark Island in the middle of the St. Lawrence River would be full of secrets, and you'd be right! Built by Frederick G. Bourne, the president of the Singer sewing machine company, at the turn of the 20th century, Singer Castle has secret passages inside its walls and grates through which you can spy on visitors (Bourne used them to hear what his guests were saying about him). Tour it today and you might even get to visit its secret dungeon.

DOGE'S PALACE
Venice, Italy

Why settle for a regular tour of this sprawling palace—once home to the rulers (or Doges) of Venice—when you can reserve a tour of the Itinerari Segreti, aka the "Secret Itineraries"? You'll get to explore hidden passageways, an interrogation room, prisons, and other parts of the palace that are off-limits during regular visits.

WARWICK CASTLE
Warwick, England

Like many European castles built in the Middle Ages, Warwick is a warren of secret passages and hidden rooms. Four such rooms—including a defensive "barbican" above the gate complete with murder holes—are now open for tours after centuries spent locked shut.

PASSETTO DI BORGO
Rome, Italy

Built over several centuries beginning in the 1200s, this 30-foot (9-m) wall contains a hidden passage that connects the Vatican to Sant'Angelo Castle, about 350 yards (320 m) away. Two popes have used the tunnel to escape sieges at various times in Vatican history. Today, visitors to Rome can tour the Passetto, which means "small passage" despite its length of more than three football fields.

PLOT THESE SPOTS FOR A VACATION TO THE UNKNOWN . . .

SNEAKY DESTINATIONS

'STACHE'S SECRET

Ninja could tell the time by looking at a cat's eye—a technique you can learn at the Ninja Museum.

NINJA MUSEUM
Iga, Japan

Located in a village that was once a center of ninja training, this museum showcases the tools and tactics of history's sneakiest warriors. Watch trained ninja wield swords, throw stars, and their own lethal hands and feet, then tour a ninja residence filled with trapdoors, fake hallways, and hidden rooms to confound intruders.

TRICK ART MUSEUM
Jeju, South Korea

Don't forget your camera—and a friend to take your photo with it—when you visit this museum of interactive illusions on Jeju Island. It features more than a hundred pieces of 3-D paintings that you become a part of when you stand, sit, or kneel in the right place.

QUEASY STREET

KURT WENNER'S "PAVEMENT ART" WILL MAKE YOUR HEAD SPIN

WHEN KURT WENNER COMES TO TOWN, WORD ON THE STREET IS "WOW!" This former NASA illustrator achieved worldwide fame for his astonishing pavement art, which creates the illusion of three-dimensional chasms, scenery, and scenarios when spotted from just the right spot. In an age of computer-generated movies and digitally doctored photos, Wenner prefers to fool the eye the old-fashioned way: with a paintbrush. Have a look at some of his groundbreaking ground paintings...

SEARCH & ENJOY: AMUSEMENT PARK SECRETS

SPELL CHECKING: Muggles mob the Wizarding World of Harry Potter in Orlando, Florida, U.S.A., to chug frosty mugs of butterbeer and spot props from the Harry Potter movies. But the best secrets here are heard and not seen. Eavesdrop at the door of the potions classroom while in line for the Forbidden Journey, a tour of Hogwarts, and you'll hear a teacher lecturing her class. Moaning Myrtle whines and wails as she haunts the bathrooms of Hogsmeade. Quiet down and listen up to detect whispering voices from the dangling ears in Zonko's Joke Shop.

HEAD GAME: Some Disney fans make it their mission to find all the Mickey Mouse heads scattered throughout the Disney parks. "Hidden Mickeys" are everywhere: painted on attraction backgrounds, chipped into sidewalks, inscribed on signs, carved in handrails, sewn into carpet patterns, and inlaid on tiled walls. Websites, guidebooks, and smartphone apps help headhunters discover them all.

COMIC RELIEF: Comic-book characters come to life at Universal Studios' Marvel Super Hero Island in Orlando, Florida, and one of the people who brought them to life left his mark throughout the park. Inspect the oversize artwork of heroes and villains and you'll spot the name of famous Marvel artist Adam Kubert. His signature is obvious in some of the drawings, but you'll have to hunt for it in others. Visitors make a game of finding the hidden Adams.

SECRET Places

SUPREMELY SNEAKY — Murder Holes

DEFINITELY DEVIOUS — El Dorado

SOLIDLY STEALTHY — Trick Art Museum

Camp Century

SLIGHTLY SHIFTY — International Spy Museum

Priest Holes

SHHH SCALE

SPECTRUM OF HUSH-HUSH HIERARCHY

Secret Agent 'Stache
Ranks SNEAKY SPOTS

CHAPTER **7**

Great Escapes and Twisted Plots

ALL THAT STANDS BETWEEN A PRISONER AND FREEDOM ARE THE STEEL BARS OF HIS OR HER CELL, thick concrete walls, and a courtyard patrolled by armed guards and watchdogs, ringed by sheer walls and barbed wire. Escape is hopeless, right? Try telling that to the men who chiseled their way out of Alcatraz, the famously inescapable prison, or the soldiers who built a glider to flee a heavily guarded castle in World War II. Desperate situations sometimes call for supreme acts of sneakiness, as you'll see in this chapter crammed with great escapes, daring schemes, and other escapades.

WINGING IT

After discovering a book on airplane design in the prison library, two prisoners and a dozen assistants spent months building a glider in the attic above the castle's chapel. Working quietly behind a false wall that hid them from patrolling guards, the men assembled the aircraft from bed parts and floorboards, wrapping it in a skin made from sleeping bags. They planned to catapult the glider from the roof to the other side of the River Mulde, using a bathtub filled with concrete as a counterweight. American soldiers liberated the prison before the glider was quite ready for takeoff. The brazen scheme became the most famous escape that never happened.

COLDITZ CASTLE COULDN'T HOLD WORLD WAR II's BREAKOUT STARS

ESCAPE

FACTORY OF PHONINESS

Sneaking beyond the castle walls was only the beginning of a "home-run" journey. Deep in enemy territory, prisoners risked rapid recapture in a countryside crawling with enemy soldiers who stopped every traveler and demanded to see "papers, please!" Escape plotters planned ahead by forging documents and disguises. They copied passes swiped from guards, creating approval stamps out of shoe rubber. They sewed civilian clothes or German uniforms to replace their prison outfits. William "Billie" Stephens, a British officer who slipped through castle windows and skulked across roofs to escape Colditz in 1941, posed as a French electrician—complete with a worker's pass—to reach the safety of Switzerland. Another escapee impersonated a German general.

SOLDIERS TAKEN PRISONER DURING WORLD WAR II MIGHT HAVE LOST THEIR BATTLES, BUT THEY COULD STILL HELP WIN THE WAR. Allied troops were under orders to escape by any means necessary, a tactic that tied up the enemy's time and resources. Prisoners even had a term for a successful getaway: a "home run." The Germans locked up the Allies' most habitual jailbreakers in Oflag IV-C, a camp walled inside a 15th-century fortress called Colditz Castle. But by imprisoning so many home-run plotters in one spot, the Germans had unwittingly created a training ground for escape artists, a sort of Hogwarts for the sneaky arts. The result: Colditz captives scored more than 30 home runs.

TUNED IN

Colditz's captives kept tabs on the outside world from a radio room hidden in the eaves of the castle. By tuning to British newscasts and reading stolen German newspapers, they were among the most informed prisoners of the war.

academy

A KEEP FOR SAFEKEEPING

The medieval castle of Colditz was built on a rocky outcrop overlooking the River Mulde near Leipzig, Germany. It served as a residence, hunting lodge, and mental hospital before the Germans turned it into a prisoner-of-war camp in 1939. Surrounded on three sides by precipitous plunges and staffed by more guards than it had captives, Colditz was deemed escape-proof.

ESCAPE ARTISTS

Oflag IV-C was home to more than 600 Allied prisoners during its run as a prison camp. They hailed from Great Britain, France, Belgium, Poland, and America, but the captives all had one thing in common: a knack for breaking out. The prisoners pooled their talents for document forgery, toolmaking, map reading, tunnel engineering, and lock picking to orchestrate escape after escape.

HOW TO BUST OUT OF "THE ROCK"

A STEP-BY-STEP GUIDE TO ESCAPING THE "INESCAPABLE" ALCATRAZ PRISON

Built on a rocky island in the middle of San Francisco Bay, battered on all sides by blood-chilling seas and treacherous tides, Alcatraz Federal Penitentiary was supposed to be an escape-proof prison for America's most hardened criminals. But that was before Frank Lee Morris, a career crook who practically grew up behind bars, stepped off the island's ferry in 1960 to become inmate #AZ-1441. He set to work masterminding an escape plan with three fellow inmates. Here's how they made their exit from Alcatraz, aka "The Rock."

STEP 1) CHIP OFF THE OLD ROCK

Using spoons and nail clippers, Morris and his co-conspirators chiseled away the concrete around ventilation grills at the backs of their cells to gain access to hidden passages in the walls. The salty air had softened the concrete, but it still took the men several months to chip through it. They replaced the missing concrete with papier-mâché so the guards wouldn't notice their progress.

ITEMS NEEDED:

Busted vacuum cleaner, rubber cement, spoons, some raincoats, an accordion, and human hair

STEP 5) SINK OR SWIM

Morris and the other men chose June 11, 1962, as the night of their escape, beginning at 9:30 p.m., shortly after lights-out (prison slang for bedtime). One escape plotter couldn't get through the ventilation grill in his cell, but the other three slipped into the hidden passageway, grabbed the rafts, and climbed to the roof through the loosened ventilation fan. Once they reached the water's edge, the men used a modified accordion to inflate the floats and set sail. Morris and the two other inmates were never seen again, leading prison officials to declare that they were swept to sea and drowned. Their bodies, however, were never found. Some speculate that inmate #AZ-1441 and his two accomplices are still at large.

STEP 2) KNOW THE DRILL

Once in the wall passage, the men skittered up pipes to reach the roof of the cell block, but their exit was still blocked by a ventilation fan. They needed to drill out the screws that held the fan in place. A broken vacuum, which one of the escape plotters volunteered to fix, provided the motor for a makeshift drill. They could only use their noisy tool during the prisoners' music practice, which covered up the drilling racket.

STEP 3) FLOAT YOUR BOAT

The men knew they couldn't swim to freedom if they managed to get outside. (In addition to its cold waters and the treacherous tides, San Francisco Bay is a habitat for great white sharks.) So they set about fashioning rafts using rubber cement and raincoats borrowed from other inmates. The rafts were stored atop the cell block until the night of the escape.

STEP 4) DEVISE SOME DECOYS

Each man crafted a papier-mâché dummy of his head using soap, toilet paper, flesh-colored paint from the art room, and hair from the prison barber shop. On the night of the escape, they tucked the phony heads into their bunks so that guards walking their rounds wouldn't notice the men missing.

Escape from prison is easy if you have...

...yoga training: A slim and slight inmate in a South Korean prison used his yoga expertise (and a tube of skin ointment) to slither through his cell door's food slot—an opening not much larger than a loaf of bread.

...locksmithing skills: Three men walked out the back door of a prison in the United Kingdom after one of them—a former sheet-metal worker—memorized the design of the guards' skeleton key and created his own.

...orange juice: A priest named John Gerard coordinated a complex escape from the Tower of London in 1597 after writing for help from accomplices on the outside. He used juice to create disappearing ink, hiding his sneaky messages from the guards.

ESCAPE ARTIST

MEET THE FOLK HERO NO PRISON COULD HOLD

MORE THAN 200 YEARS BEFORE THE BEATLES, JACK SHEPPARD WAS THE CLOSEST THING ENGLAND HAD TO A ROCK STAR. A carpenter by day in the early 1700s, Sheppard spent his nights burglarizing the homes of his clients. But these common crimes weren't the source of his celebrity. When the long arm of the law grabbed Sheppard four times, he managed to wiggle free in a series of famous escapes, each more daring than the last. At just 22 years old, he became England's most wanted man—and its biggest star.

'STACHE'S SECRET

After his third escape, Jack Sheppard wrote a mocking apology letter to the executioner. "I am now drinking [to] your health," he assured the hangman.

FIRST ESCAPE: UP AND AWAY

Turned in by his brother, a fellow thief, in 1724, Sheppard was locked overnight on the top floor of St. Giles Roundhouse, a jail for small-fry crooks. Wasting no time hacking a hole through the roundhouse's wooden roof, Sheppard clambered to the ground on a rope fashioned from bedclothes. The racket of his escape attracted a crowd, so he distracted them by shouting that the escapee was still on the roof. The diversion actually worked! Concealing his manacles, Sheppard blended with the gawkers and moseyed into the night.

SECOND ESCAPE: TWO TO GO

Sheppard was arrested for pickpocketing just a month later, and this time he ran into an old flame in jail. Convincing their captors that they were a married couple, the two were transferred to New Prison, where they were both chained to the floor of a cell together. An acquaintance smuggled Sheppard a cutting tool during a prison visit. It took him only a few days to file through his and his girlfriend's manacles. They loosened a bar in the window to create an escape hatch, then climbed down yet another rope of sheets and clothes. The duo sneaked through the courtyard and scaled the prison's 22-foot (6.7-m) gate to freedom.

THIRD ESCAPE: LADIES' MAN

By July 1724, word of Sheppard's escape artistry had gone viral, whispered among the working classes and spread throughout the criminal underground. When he was arrested again for burglary in July—and this time sentenced to death—he had the people on his side. Sheppard was locked in London's Newgate Prison, home to some of England's most notorious prisoners. In late August, two of Sheppard's female friends paid him a visit. While they distracted the guards, Sheppard managed to remove a bar from the window and slip his trim frame through the gap. His friends quickly dolled him up in women's clothing, and the three left Newgate together.

FINAL ESCAPE: SHEPPARD'S BIG BREAK

By this point, Sheppard had become a sensation for thumbing his nose at England's brutal authorities. To the people in charge, however, he was big trouble. You better believe they took extra measures to secure Sheppard for the hangman's noose when he was recaptured in September. They locked him in an especially secure Newgate Prison cell known as the "castle." He was shackled in manacles, his leg irons padlocked to the floor. It wasn't enough. In October, Sheppard used a nail to pick the locks, then pulled an iron bar from a chimney in his cell. Still hobbled by leg irons, Sheppard used the bar to break through no less than six heavily secured doors before reaching the roof of the prison. He climbed atop a neighboring house, tiptoed down its stairs without waking the residents with his clanking chains, and escaped into the night and the countryside.

NO ESCAPE

The escape artist's luck eventually ran out. Despite warnings from friends and his own mother, who wanted him to flee the country, Sheppard couldn't resist the call of the city and a life of crime. He was captured on November 1, 1724, and held under 24-hour guard until the date of his execution. More than 200,000 people—nearly a third of London's population—turned out to see if Sheppard could give the slip to the hangman's noose. He nearly did. A last-minute search revealed a knife hidden in his clothing. He was planning to cut his bonds and escape into the crowd. Without a doubt, they would have helped him.

BUSY BODY

BODY

'STACHE'S SECRET

Cholmondeley and Montagu worked for the "Twenty Committee," the British intelligence team in charge of recruiting double agents. The Committee's name was inspired by the Roman numerals XX, or "double cross." Clever, huh?

THE BURIAL PLOT THAT HELPED WIN A WAR

Operation Mincemeat had all the drama and derring-do of a Hollywood movie. In fact, its events were depicted in 1956's *The Man Who Never Was*. In the scene above, our deceased hero is deployed on his secret mission.

MAJOR WILLIAM MARTIN OF THE BRITISH ROYAL MARINES MANAGED TO SNEAK BEHIND ENEMY LINES, fool one of Germany's top spies, and clear the way for an Allied invasion in World War II.

Not bad for a dead guy.

Martin wasn't some zombie super-soldier. He was the central figure in "Operation Mincemeat," one of the most successful deceptions in the history of sneaky warfare. William Martin wasn't even his real name. His identity—and the entire operation—was devised in 1943 by two cunning English intelligence officers, Charles Cholmondeley and Ewen Montagu. Their big idea: Find a recently deceased man who looked like he had perished at sea, dress him in a British military uniform, equip him with secret—but bogus—military documents, and set him adrift so the Germans would find him. Pulling it off required a vast cast of characters, intense planning, and loads of luck.

After tracking down the perfect corpse (Welshman Glyndwr Michael) and renaming

him William Martin, the two officers set about giving the body a life of his own. They filled his wallet and pockets with personal letters and receipts, fake IDs, and photos. They even included a picture of Martin's phony fiancée, Pam (actually a clerk in their office). With his background built, Martin was ready for his most essential accessory—a briefcase full of military plans for a phony invasion of

Greece, handcuffed to his wrist. Sealed in a casket of dry ice to stave off rot, Major Martin was ready for his mission.

A Royal Navy submarine dumped Martin near the port of Huelva, Spain, home of a notorious German spy named Adolf Clauss. A local fisherman found Martin, and soon the body and his briefcase caught Clauss' attention. When Spanish authorities returned Martin's body to the British, it was clear that the secret documents had been seen. Intelligence officials dispatched a message to British Prime Minister Winston Churchill, who had been following the operation: "Mincemeat swallowed whole."

German leaders—including Adolf Hitler—fell for the trick. They deployed their troops to the decoy invasion point detailed in the phony documents. That left Sicily, site of the real invasion, lightly defended. Countless Allied forces were spared from a brutal battle. And all because of the bobbing body of a made-up major named William Martin.

THREE PLOTS SO CRAZY... THEY ACTUALLY WORKED!

Movie Magic

When the Central Intelligence Agency needed to rescue six Americans from Iran in 1980, the spy agency concocted an escape plan right out of a movie—literally! Tony Mendez, a CIA master of disguise and expert at exfiltration (remember that word from the spy chapter?), devised bogus identities for the six Americans: that of a Canadian film crew scouting for movie locations. To give the story credibility, he set up a fake studio office in Hollywood and placed ads for a phony science-fiction film called *Argo* in Hollywood publications. Mendez then flew to Iran and delivered the fake identification documents to the Americans, who were hiding out in the home of the Canadian ambassador. Posing as members of the Canadian film crew, the Americans boarded a plane and escaped the country. The audacious rescue—which became known as the "Canadian Caper"—was later portrayed in a real Hollywood movie, 2012's *Argo*.

Mailed Man

While many slaves during the American Civil War used the Underground Railroad—a vast network of secret routes and safe houses—to sneak to freedom in the north, Henry "Box" Brown concocted his own escape plan by thinking outside the box. Or, rather, inside it. Brown, born a slave in North Carolina, asked a carpenter in 1849 to build a wooden crate 3 feet long by 2 feet wide (0.9 m by 0.6 m). After poking ventilation holes and packing some water, Brown squeezed into the box and had friends nail it shut. They mailed this very special delivery to the Anti-Slavery Society in Philadelphia, Pennsylvania, U.S.A. The trip took more than a day, and Brown spent most of it upside down (despite writing "right side up with care" on the box's outside). He arrived safely and became active in Philadelphia's antislavery movement.

AND TWO PLOTS **SO CRAZY** . . . THEY DIDN'T WORK!

Remote-Control Kitty

In the 1960s, researchers at the Central Intelligence Agency spent millions of dollars trying to turn a cat into a slinking, battery-operated cyber kitty that could eavesdrop on the conversations of Soviet officials. They surgically implanted a cat—dubbed "Acoustic Kitty"—with a microphone in her ear, a transmitter in her skull, and an antenna in her tail. In trial runs, the cat wandered off to chase mice, so the researchers figured out how to curb Acoustic Kitty's appetite. Unfortunately, she proved hard to train and was run over by a taxi on her first real mission. Which begs the question: Why didn't the CIA try an Acoustic Canine?

The (Almost) Great Escape

While Colditz Castle's captives plotted their getaways one at a time or in small groups, a much more ambitious escape plan was coming together in the German prisoner-of-war camp known as Stalag Luft III. British pilot Roger Bushell masterminded a plot to sneak more than 200 prisoners out of the camp through three secret tunnels named Tom, Dick, and Harry. More than 600 soldiers dug the tunnels, hiding the dirt in their pockets and relying on homemade pumps for fresh air. On the night of the escape in 1944, only 77 prisoners made it through Harry before the guards caught on. All but three were recaptured. The Germans executed 50 of the escapees—including Bushell—as a lesson to other prisoners.

Ghost Army

Tanks clashed and artillery blasted across the battlefields of World War II, but for the 1,100 men of the 23rd Headquarters Special Troops, it was all a big game of pretend. This contingent of artists and actors, special-effects experts, and set designers was tasked with staging battles using blow-up tanks and jeeps, wooden cannons, and phony planes on painted runways. Audio engineers blared the sounds of skirmishes—explosions, screaming tank engines, and infantry commands—from speakers across the bogus battlefield, while radio operators broadcast phony chatter. What was the point of all this pretend combat? To convince the German army that a 30,000-man Allied force was in their midst, thus distracting their attention from real soldiers and vehicles. The 23rd logged 21 operations, some so successful that German soldiers surrendered to the dummy tanks!

CYBER SCAVENGER HUNT

A CRYPTIC TRIP THROUGH THE INTERNET'S DARKEST DOMAINS

'STACHE'S SECRET

If the CIA really is behind Cicada 3301, it wouldn't be the first time an intelligence agency created a recruitment test. The U.S. Cyber Command hid a code in one of its logos in 2010 and challenged the public to crack it.

Cicada Suspects

WHO'S BEHIND 3301'S CRYPTIC QUEST?

THE MESSAGE WAS SHORT AND SIMPLE, EMBEDDED IN AN IMAGE OF GLOWING TEXT AGAINST A DARK BACKGROUND IN AN ONLINE MESSAGE FORUM. "Hello," it began. "We are looking for highly intelligent individuals. To find them, we have devised a test. There is a message hidden in this image. Find it, and it will lead you on the road to finding us... Good luck." And so began the Internet's most cryptic quest, a sequence of puzzles that lured thousands of web wonks to the Net's nether reaches and even into the real world. The message was signed not with a name but a number: 3301.

Hackers, amateur code crackers, and other intrepid Internet explorers took up the challenge, working alone or together in private forums. Within hours of the message's appearance on January 5, 2012, many had decoded a Caesar's cipher (see page 168) hidden within the image, which led to more puzzles and clues. Each test required a different expertise: mathematics, music, Maya numbers, literature, programming. Solving a puzzle incorrectly could lead to false clues that threw the unworthy off the trail. Eventually, the tests led to a Texas, U.S.A., phone number and an answering machine, which in turn led to a website with a countdown clock and a large picture of a cicada insect. The cicada had become the symbol of the quest now known as "Cicada 3301."

When the clock reached zero on January 9, 2012, the site revealed 14 coordinates on three continents. Questers fanned out to inspect the spots, which turned out to be lampposts bearing secret codes pointing to a murky region of the web known as the "darknet." Uncharted by search engines, the darknet is the Internet's seedy underbelly, home to gigabytes of unsavory data and secret networks that want to stay that way. No one knows how many Cicada 3301 participants managed to navigate the darknet to take the prize. A final message—supposedly from the mysterious plotters of the puzzle—surfaced in February 2012. "We have now found the individuals we sought," it read. "Thus our month-long journey ends." In the end, the prize in this scavenger hunt wasn't money or gadgets or even bragging rights. It was the savvy few who could solve the riddle of Cicada 3301.

THE CIA: Did America's spy agency set up Cicada as a recruitment tool?

ANONYMOUS: Perhaps Cicada was an initiation for this secretive collective of "hacker activists."

A GAME COMPANY: Video-game companies have created elaborate "alternate-reality games" to promote their releases in the past.

UNBELIEVABLE!

THE **"PROOF"** AND **TRUTH** BEHIND THREE KOOKY **CONSPIRACY** THEORIES

THE MOON LANDING WAS PHONY!

Original moonwalkers Neil Armstrong and Buzz Aldrin made history when they became the first astronauts to stroll on the lunar surface in 1969, but conspiracy theorists insist the landing was one giant lie instead of "one giant leap" for mankind. They claim that NASA secretly filmed the mission on a hidden Hollywood set to convince the Soviet Union that the U.S. had won the space race to the moon.

THE "PROOF": Landing deniers point to NASA footage of Aldrin planting the American flag in the lunar soil. A subtle wiggle in the flag fabric, they say, proves that it blew in the wind—which doesn't exist in the vacuum of space.

THE TRUTH: NASA claims the flag only wiggled because Aldrin was twisting it into the moon's surface. The astronauts also returned with rocks and soil samples verified to be of lunar origin.

ALIENS CRASHED IN ROSWELL!

A rancher discovered the wreckage of an unidentified flying object (UFO) near the small town of Roswell, New Mexico, U.S.A., in 1947. Linking it to a recent rash of flying-saucer sightings, he reported the debris to the sheriff, who in turn called the nearby Roswell Army Air Field (RAAF). The military confiscated the wreckage, claiming it was a weather balloon, but conspiracy theorists later accused the government of hushing up a UFO crash. They believe the alien ship and the bodies of its pilots were spirited away to Area 51, the top secret government base in the Nevada desert.

THE "PROOF": In the 1970s, supposed eyewitnesses to the Roswell crash began coming forward to claim they saw tiny alien corpses recovered from the wreckage. Others insisted the debris contained impossibly strong metal alloys not of this world. At least one former Air Force officer swore there was not one, but two crashes.

THE TRUTH: The U.S. government released a report in the mid-1990s to put Roswell's conspiracies to rest. The report revealed that the 1947 debris was actually a crashed balloon in its top secret "Project Mogul," which used high-altitude sensors to monitor for enemy nuclear-missile tests. The "alien corpses" were crash-test dummies dropped from miles in the sky to test parachute technology.

EXTRATERRESTRIAL REPTILES CONTROL THE WORLD!

According to those who believe in the "reptilian elite," humanity's most powerful people aren't people at all. Our politicians, movie stars, pop singers, and billionaire executives are actually members of a race of cold-blooded extraterrestrial reptiles called the Annunaki, who voyaged from the constellation Draco long ago to enslave humanity. Working behind the scenes, these lizard overlords orchestrate wars and natural disasters to sow global grouchiness, which to them is a sort of energy.

THE "PROOF": English author, conspiracy theorist, and former pro soccer player David Icke wrote about the reptile elite in 1998 in his first book, *The Biggest Secret*. In it he laid out the Annunaki's hidden history on Earth and their experiments in crossbreeding with humans to create a new race. The book contained interviews with supposed eyewitnesses to reptilians finagling with global events. And don't bother looking for scaly tails or slitted pupils on your favorite movie stars: The Annunaki can assume human shape to blend in with the locals. Search the Internet and you'll find plenty of (obviously Photoshopped) images of famous people accidentally revealing their reptilian side.

THE TRUTH: Icke's theory of shape-changing aliens is conveniently hard to disprove—especially to anyone already prone to distrusting the powers that be. Still, you have to think it's pretty silly that Queen Elizabeth is secretly a crowned lizard lady from some dragon-shaped constellation.

'STACHE'S SECRET

The American Southwest is a hotbed of UFO conspiracies. Aside from Roswell and Area 51, it's also allegedly home to "Dulce Base," a supposed secret subterranean facility buzzing with recovered alien technology on the border of Colorado and New Mexico.

SKULL AND BONES: Despite its scary name—and the fact that its members meet in a secretive hall called the "Tomb"—Skull and Bones isn't some sinister organization. It's an exclusive social club formed by students at Yale University in 1832. Members (called "Bonesmen") include former presidents, Supreme Court justices, famous writers, movie stars, and captains of industry. Conspiracy theorists claim that Skull and Bones membership is a first step to becoming a spy for the Central Intelligence Agency—a claim that the CIA denies.

Skull and Bones
FOUNDED 1832

322

THE FREEMASONS: It's one of the world's oldest and largest fraternities, but the freemasons don't have a website or advertise for new members. Instead, potential initiates must earn an invitation from high-ranking Freemasons and commit to memory elaborate rituals. This ancient men's club spawned in the Middle Ages as a professional organization for skilled carvers of stone (although some believe they originated from ancient druids or a mysterious group of warriors called the Knights Templar). Freemason ranks include George Washington and composer Wolfgang Amadeus Mozart.

THE ILLUMINATI: The most secretive of secret societies, the Illuminati (the Latin word for "enlightened") has its roots in an 18th-century German sect that rejected superstition and embraced the pursuit of knowledge. It was quickly disbanded, but the Illuminati lives on in conspiracy theories as a shadowy organization that controls everything from presidential elections to the outcome of the next World Series.

PLOT
Points

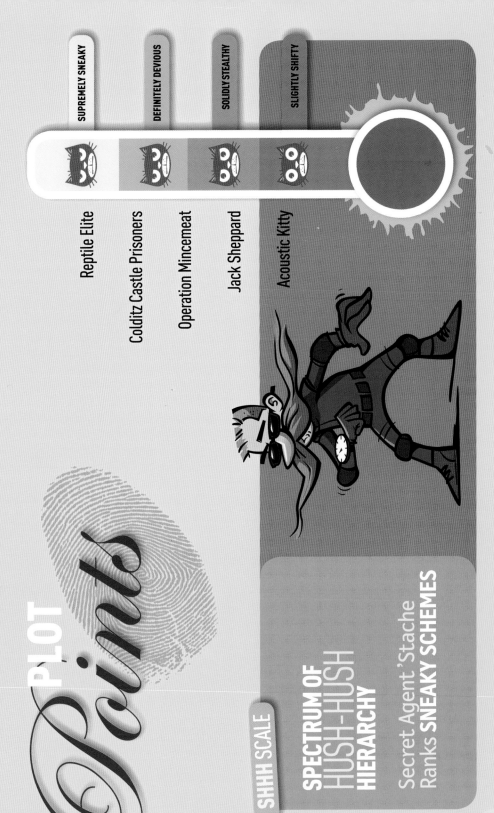

SUPREMELY SNEAKY	Reptile Elite
DEFINITELY DEVIOUS	Colditz Castle Prisoners
SOLIDLY STEALTHY	Operation Mincemeat
	Jack Sheppard
SLIGHTLY SHIFTY	Acoustic Kitty

SHHH SCALE

SPECTRUM OF HUSH-HUSH HIERARCHY

Secret Agent 'Stache Ranks **SNEAKY SCHEMES**

153

CHAPTER 8

Sneaky Fun

IT'S A FACT CONFIRMED EACH TIME YOU STEAL SECOND BASE OR WIN A ROUND OF HIDE-AND-SEEK: BEING SNEAKY IS A BLAST!

That's why this final chapter is crammed with top secret activities and adventures that engage your undercover instincts. Learn to communicate in code, mix invisible ink, track hidden animals, master magic tricks, and more. Just be careful who sneaks a peek. This chapter is for your eyes only!

SEEK THE Sneaks

CAN YOU FIND THE CAMOUFLAGED CREATURES HIDING IN THESE SCENES?

1

DID YOU FIND ME?
1: Lion hiding in the tall grass in the upper left of the photo.
2: Katydid holding on to the branch. I am the thing you think is a leaf!
3: Bird hiding in the tall grass at the edge of the water in the dead center.
4: Moth hiding atop a stack of leaves in the dead center.
5: Spider hiding inside a sunflower in the upper middle of the flower.

THE ABC'S OF ABRACADABRA

ESSENTIAL TRICKS FOR THE STARTING SORCERER

THE PINKIE BREAK

ESSENTIAL FOR: CARD TRICKS

Before you start asking people to "pick a card, any card," you need to know this fundamental trick for marking a spot in the deck. Why is deck marking so crucial? It will help you find and retrieve any card slipped back into the deck by audience members. Here's a breakdown of the pinkie break, complete with a trick to illustrate its potential. . . .

DIRECTIONS

STEP 1) While holding the deck face down in your dominant hand and fanning it open, ask an audience member to choose a card at random.

STEP 2) Ask the audience member to memorize the card, then slip it back into your deck in a random spot. Hold the deck tight so the chosen card sticks out a little bit.

STEP 3) Here's where the pinkie break comes into play. With your free hand, split the deck above the card that was chosen by the audience member. Fit the card flush with the rest of the deck beneath it, then place the top half of the deck onto the audience member's card, while sticking the tip of your deck hand's pinkie in between the two halves of the deck. This will create a break—the pinkie break!—between the cards on top of the audience member's card.

STEP 4) Cut the deck a few times to give the impression that you're shuffling. Create a new pinkie break each time you place cards on top of the audience member's card. Keeping a sneaky pinkie break isn't easy, so make sure to practice, practice, practice!

STEP 5) When you're ready to reveal the audience member's card, cut the deck above the pinkie break, which will put the chosen card on top. Reveal the card to your audience and bask in the stunned stares and applause.

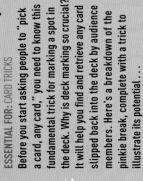

1.

2.

3.

4.

5.

 **1.**

 2.

 3.

 4.

5.

COIN PALM

ESSENTIAL FOR: VANISHING TRICKS

Your success as a magician depends on your mastery of "sleight of hand," or the ability to manipulate objects in such sneaky ways that the audience can't tell what you're doing. The coin palm is a classic example. Do it right, and you can make coins vanish right before your audience's eyes. It's also good practice for more complicated sleight-of-hand tricks—and you might earn a few bucks' worth of "disappearing quarters" in the process. Prepare to follow the palming plan . . .

Directions

STEP 1] Look at your dominant hand while moving your thumb inward slightly. See how flexing that tiny muscle creates a crease and a pocket in the center of your palm? That's where your coin will "disappear."

STEP 2] Ask for a coin from your audience. Larger coins such as dollars and half dollars will be easier for beginners to palm. Plus, they're worth more if you decide to never make them reappear.

STEP 3] Place the coin in the center of your dominant hand palm up, then shift your thumb to create that little crease mentioned in step one. If done right, the crease will lock the coin in the center of your palm. Practice until you have this step down.

STEP 4] Turn your hand with the coin upside down. Voila! The coin is still locked to your palm. Make a big deal of showing your audience that your other hand is empty.

STEP 5] You have many options for magic tricks once you have the coin successfully palmed. You can drop it into your opposite hand while passing your hands over one another, or drop it into your lap while no one is looking, then hold both palms up to show that you've made the coin disappear. You can pretend to pull the coin from someone's nose or ear. The more you practice, the more trick possibilities will come to you.

MIMIC OR MONSTER?

GUESS WHICH CREATURE IN EACH PAIR OF PICTURES IS THE HARMLESS MIMIC

4

5

MIMICRY KEY

1] Left, the Allobates zaparo frog is a mimic of the poison-dart frog on the right.

2] Left, the metalmark moth mimics its predator the jumping spider on the right.

3] Right, the hoverfly is a mimic of the bee on the left.

4] Left, the milk snake is a mimic of the deadly coral snake on the right.

5] Right, the ash borer moth mimics the wasp on the left.

HAPPY HUNTING!

HOW TO SET UP A SCAVENGER HUNT ... WITH A SNEAKY TWIST!

SOMETIMES THE BEST "TREASURES" AREN'T REALLY TREASURES AT ALL. THEY MIGHT BE PICTURES OR TASKS OR TRINKETS THAT HAVE SIGNIFICANCE ONLY TO YOU AND YOUR BUDDIES. This sort of secret stuff makes the perfect subject of a scavenger hunt, a type of game in which teams compete to see who can complete a list of objectives for points or to see who can complete them all first. It's also the perfect contest to show off sneaky skills! Here's your guide to a successful scavenger-hunting season.

'STACHE'S SECRET

You think the sample scavenger-hunt objectives suggested here are silly? Students at the University of Chicago throw a hunt that never fails to make the papers. Each annual event takes months of planning and consists of hundreds of objectives, such as building a bridge over a campus pond (worth 60 points) and setting up a meeting with the mayor of Chicago (worth just 25 points).

STEP 1) **Pick a place to host your hunt. Your backyard, a public park, a nature walk, the mall, an amusement park—any place with room to roam will do. You can theme your hunt around your chosen location or choose the location based on your theme.**

STEP 2) **Come up with a prize for the winners of the hunt. It can be anything from a bag of candy to plain old bragging rights to a trophy you design yourself!**

STEP 3) **Create the list of "treasures" for your hunters to scavenge. Keep it simple at first: a Hula-Hoop, a pair of socks, a Lego block, etc. Feel free to assign points to the objectives based on their difficulty.**

STEP 4) **Invite some friends to play the game. Divide them into teams. Each team should have no more than four people. The more players you have, the more teams you need.**

STEP 5) **Play a few simple games until you get the hang of things. The winner is the team that completes their list first (or wins the most points if you scored the objectives based on difficulty).**

STEP 6) **Get creative! Why make your contestants find a Hula-Hoop when you can make them use the hoop for five minutes in the front yard? Why send them after a single Lego block when you can make them build a robot with it? (The best robot gets bonus points.) Here are some other silly ideas for inspiration . . .**
• Sing a pop song at a bus stop. Record the performance on a digital camera or phone.
• Snap camera photos of a bird in a tree, another bird in flight, and a third bird on the ground.
• Strike a pose with a statue for a photo.
• Order Mexican food in Spanish.

STEP 7) **The best part about inventing a game is playtesting it! Try out your silliest objectives on your closest friends, then revamp the hunt list until your scavenger hunts become the social event of the neighborhood. Most important of all, have fun!**

SNEAKING UP CLOSE!

2

4

1

3

ANSWERS: 1. *Tibetan mastiff* 2. *eastern screech owl* 3. *shoe transmitter* 4. *Trojan Horse* 5. *Indo-Malayan mimic octopus* 6. *fake dragon skull*

Can you identify these six creatures or objects—all of which were featured earlier in the book—from their extremely sneaky close-ups? *(Answers at the bottom of the page.)*

CREATE SNEAKY INK

RECIPE 1: **SOUR SOAKER**
REQUIRED ITEMS: Lemon juice, cotton swabs, and a heat source such as a lightbulb (halogen won't work)

DIRECTIONS
STEP 1) **Squeeze a lemon into a bowl and add a little water, or use store-bought lemon juice instead.**

STEP 2) **Dip the head of a cotton swab into the lemon juice.**

STEP 3) **Use the swab like a pen to mark your message on a white piece of paper. Apply more juice to the swab if it dries out, but don't soak it or your paper will become a soggy mess.**

STEP 4) **Allow the paper to dry, then pass it to the person you want to communicate with secretly.**

STEP 5) **To reveal the message, carefully hold the paper in front of a heat source such as a lightbulb or even the sun. Never place the paper on the bulb or it might catch fire. Your hidden message will reveal itself in brown letters.**

RECIPE 2: **PURPLE POWER**
REQUIRED ITEMS: Baking soda, grape juice (from concentrate is fine), cotton swab

DIRECTIONS
STEP 1) **Mix equal amounts of baking soda and water in a small cup.**

STEP 2) **Dip your swab in the solution, then use it to write your message on a white piece of paper.**

STEP 3) **Allow the paper to dry, then pass it to the person you want to communicate with secretly.**

STEP 4) **To reveal the message, use a sponge or brush to paint the paper with purple grape juice. The slight acidity of the grape juice reacts with the baking soda to reveal your message on the page.**

EMAILS GET LEFT OPEN. GOSSIPY SIBLINGS READ TEXT MESSAGES OVER YOUR SHOULDER. YOUR PERSONAL LIFE IS AN OPEN BOOK IF YOU DON'T TAKE PRECAUTIONS. The only surefire method of secret communication is to write with old-fashioned invisible ink. A good spy never repeats his or her tactics, so we've supplied three ink recipes that will keep enemy agents—and nosy classmates—guessing ...

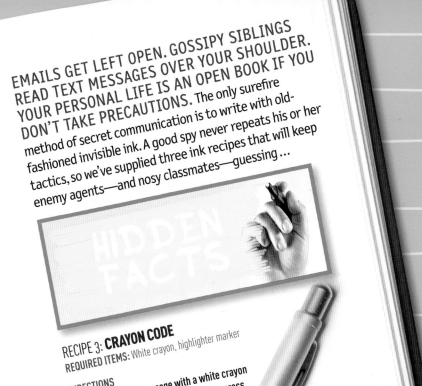

HIDDEN FACTS

RECIPE 3: **CRAYON CODE**
REQUIRED ITEMS: White crayon, highlighter marker

DIRECTIONS
STEP 1) **Write your message with a white crayon on a white piece of paper. Make sure to press firmly with the crayon.**

STEP 2) **Pass the paper to the person you want to communicate with secretly.**

STEP 3) **To reveal the message, go over the page with a high-lighter marker until your crayon code stands out.**

'STACHE'S SECRET
Passing a blank piece of paper to your agents might arouse suspicion, so heed this tip from an old pro: Write a harmless note in regular ink on the same paper to give your secret message a little extra cover.

CODEBUSTERS!

Memorize these "CIPHERS" to communicate in secret.

Secret messages aren't just for spies and baseball pitchers. Anyone can concoct a cryptic code with the help of a cipher: a system for replacing or rearranging letters in the alphabet to conceal messages. Think of a cipher as the key to locking and unlocking your secret code. As long as all the spies in your network know how the cipher works, they can read every secret order dispatched from your underground lair.

What's that? You don't have a spy network? Well that'll be step one. Recruit your friends, your siblings—maybe even your crazy Aunt Edna—then choose one of the classic ciphers below to begin broadcasting intel in secret. Finding an underground lair, however, is up to you.

THE CAESAR CIPHER

Named for Roman ruler Julius Caesar (who used it in his private letters), the Caesar cipher relies on a simple shift in the letters of the alphabet by a set number of spaces left or right. For example, if you set your Caesar cipher to shift three spaces right, A then becomes D, B becomes E, G becomes J, etc., in your coded alphabet. Only people who know your cipher can crack the code. Here's how your cipher-shifted alphabet looks compared to the regular alphabet . . .

CAESAR CIPHER: D E F G H I J K L M N O P Q R S T U V W X Y Z A B C
REGULAR ALPHABET: A B C D E F G H I J K L M N O P Q R S T U V W X Y Z

Using this cipher, the message "calling all spies" would encrypt as "fdoolqj doo vslhv."

DECODE THE CODE!

Try out your new decrypting skills on these secret messages. Each one uses a cipher explained on this page.

1) Yjr d;urdy d[ord eom yjr [toxr

2) Xltp elukp dq nhlvj

3) Wuxvw qr rqh

ANSWERS
1) The slyest spies win the prize
(created using the keyboard cipher)
2) Your cover is blown
(created using the keyword cipher with "sneaky" as the keyword)
3) Trust no one
(created using the Caesar cipher right three.)

THE **KEYBOARD** CIPHER

This cipher is a cinch to use for anyone familiar with a computer keyboard. Simply place your fingers on the keys as you normally would, then shift your fingers one space to the right. Begin typing your message, which will appear as gibberish to everyone but your agents. They'll know you're using the keyboard cipher, and they can decode your message by looking at a computer keyboard and looking at each letter to the left.

Using this cipher, the message "calling all spies" would encrypt as "vs;;omh s;; d[ord." (Look at the letter to the left of these letters on a keyboard to see how the cipher works.)

THE **KEYWORD** CIPHER

This one's a little more complicated—perfect for super-duper top secret orders to agents under deep cover (close friends of your secret crush, for instance). First, you need to choose a keyword; any weird word will do, but it cannot have any repeating letters. For this example, we'll go with "sneaky." Now write your keyword down, then write the alphabet after it in normal order while also removing any letters that appear in the keyword. Print the normal alphabet above or below your keyword alphabet as a guide for your secret missives, like this:

KEYWORD ALPHABET: S N E A K Y B C D F G H I J L M O P Q R T U V W X Z
REGULAR ALPHABET: A B C D E F G H I J K L M N O P Q R S T U V W X Y Z

Using this cipher, the message "calling all spies" would become "eshhdjb shh qmdkq."

REAL PHOTO or PHOTOSHOP?

**PICK THE
REAL PICTURES
FROM THE
DOCTORED ONES**

1

2

3

ANSWERS: 1: Real photo of pro surfer Garrett McNamara riding a 100-foot (30.5-m) wave off the coast of Portugal. **2:** Fake **3:** Real photo taken in a desert in Namibia, Africa. The morning light mixed with the sand dunes behind the trees give the picture a painted look. **4:** Fake **5:** Fake **6:** Real photo of St. Maarten's Maho beach, famous for its jet-blasted location on the landing path for passenger planes at Princess Juliana International Airport. **7:** Fake

UNFAIR PLAY
THE WORLD'S SNEAKIEST JOCKS

FOUL BALL: Any game that allows theft—in baseball's case, stealing bases—is bound to encourage some underhanded athletics. And no baseball strategy is sneakier than the classic "hidden ball trick." It works like this: Shortly after a base run, the baseman closest to the runner pretends to toss the ball back to the pitcher (while actually hiding it in his or her glove or armpit). The moment the runner steps off the base—tag!—he or she is out! Boston's Marty Barrett was the master of this sneaky trick, pulling it off three times in the mid-1980s.

SPEED DEMONS: Stock-car racing was started by troublemaking grease monkeys who souped up their cars to outrun police, so it's no surprise that drivers are eager to bend the rules today. Although all cars in a race are supposed to meet the same specifications, drivers and their teams will often add secret upgrades. One driver famously loaded the frame of his car with ball bearings so that it would meet NASCAR's weight requirements. He dumped them through a trap-door once on the track to lighten his car and boost his top speed. The hailstorm of tiny metal balls on the pit crews gave him away.

HANDY MAN: Everyone knows that football—aka "soccer" in the United States and Canada—is a hands-off sport for all the players except the goalies. But apparently the rules didn't apply to Argentine pro Diego Maradona, considered one of the sport's greatest athletes. While playing in a World Cup quarter-final match against England in 1986, Maradona spiked the ball into the goal with one hand while making it look like he used his head. The referee missed the penalty, and Maradona's team went on to win the World Cup. Known as "the hand of God," Maradona's dirty trick is one of the most famous sneak plays in sports history.

TOUR DE FARCE: Just as NASCAR drivers tweak their engines with illegal upgrades to get an edge on the competition, professional cyclists have been known to soup up their own engines—their bodies. Some high-profile riders have been caught using performance-enhancing substances to increase their endurance and pedaling power during the Tour de France and other grueling long-distance races.

FAST AND CURIOUS: Marathon runner Rosie Ruiz had a clever strategy for finishing the 1980 Boston Marathon with a record time: She took the subway. Suspicious of such a spectacular performance from an unknown runner (Ruiz's finish was the third fastest in women's marathon history), officials scrutinized photos from the race and didn't see Ruiz in any until the very end. It turns out she merely registered for the marathon and sneaked in through the crowd just one mile (1.6 km) from the end.

Secret Agent 'Stache
BIDS
farewell

Well, kiddo, I'm afraid I've run dry of classified facts and secret information. Consider me impressed by your curiosity! In fact, I think I'm going to start my own super-duper secret branch of the Professional Sleuths of Super-Secret Truths, and you're my first agent. Here's your badge, kid. Now get out there and put your sneaky skills to the test. The new P.S.S.S.T. needs more secrets!

INDEX

Boldface indicates illustrations.

CREDITS

Dedicated to Mike Price,
an old partner in paranormal investigations
and a fearless friend in spooky places. —CB

Published by the National Geographic Society
Gary E. Knell, *President and Chief Executive Officer*
John M. Fahey, *Chairman of the Board*
Declan Moore, *Executive Vice President; President,*
    Publishing and Travel
Melina Gerosa Bellows, *Publisher; Chief Creative*
    Officer, Books, Kids, and Family

Prepared by the Book Division
Hector Sierra, *Senior Vice President and General*
    Manager
Nancy Laties Feresten, *Senior Vice President, Kids*
    Publishing and Media
Eva Absher-Schantz, *Design Director, Kids Publishing*
    and Media
Jay Sumner, *Director of Photography, Kids Publishing*
Jennifer Emmett, *Vice President, Editorial Director,*
    Kids Books
R. Gary Colbert, *Production Director*
Jennifer A. Thornton, *Director of Managing Editorial*

Staff for This Book
Becky Baines, *Senior Editor*
Jim Hiscott, *Art Director*
John Foster, *Designer*
Jay Sumner, *Photo Editor*
Kris Hanneman, *Photo Researcher*
Paige Towler, *Editorial Assistant*
Michael Libonati, *Special Projects Assistant*
Sanjida Rashid, *Design Production Assistant*
Margaret Leist, *Photo Assistant*
Grace Hill, *Associate Managing Editor*
Joan Gossett, *Production Editor*
Lewis R. Bassford, *Production Manager*
Susan Borke, *Legal and Business Affairs*

Production Services
Phillip L. Schlosser, *Senior Vice President*
Chris Brown, *Vice President, NG Book Manufacturing*
George Bounelis, *Senior Production Manager*
Nicole Elliott, *Director of Production*
Robert L. Barr, *Manager*
Darrick D. McRae, *Imaging Technician*

The National Geographic
Society is one of the
world's largest nonprofit
scientific and educational
organizations. Founded in
1888 to "increase and diffuse
geographic knowledge," the
member-supported Society
works to inspire people to care about the planet.
Through its online community, members can get
closer to explorers and photographers, connect with
other members around the world and help make a
difference. National Geographic reflects the world
through its magazines, television programs, films,
books, DVDs, radio, maps, exhibitions, live events,
school publishing programs, interactive media and
merchandise. *National Geographic* magazine, the
Society's official journal, published in English and
39 local-language editions, is read by more than 60
million people each month. The National Geographic
Channel reaches 440 million households in 171
countries in 48 languages. National Geographic
Digital Media receives more than 27 million visitors
a month. National Geographic has funded more than
10,000 scientific research, conservation and exploration projects and supports an education program
promoting geographic literacy.

For more information, please visit
nationalgeographic.com,
call 1-800-NGS LINE (647-5463),
or write to the following address:
National Geographic Society
1145 17th Street N.W.
Washington, D.C. 20036-4688 U.S.A.

Visit us online at nationalgeographic.com/books

For librarians and teachers: ngchildrensbooks.org

More for kids from National Geographic:
kids.nationalgeographic.com

For information about special discounts for bulk
purchases, please contact National Geographic
Books Special Sales: ngspecsales@ngs.org

For rights or permissions inquiries, please contact
National Geographic Books Subsidiary Rights:
ngbookrights@ngs.org

Paperback ISBN: 978-1-4263-1783-5
Reinforced library binding ISBN: 978-1-4263-1784-2

Printed in Hong Kong
14/THK/1